MW00604273

The Reluctant Rainmaker:
A Guide for Lawyers Who Hate Selling

Julie A. Fleming, J.D.

Atlanta

The Reluctant Rainmaker: A Guide for Lawyers Who Hate Selling
by Julie A. Fleming, J.D.

All rights reserved. No part of this book may be reproduced in any means, print or electronic, without consent of: Julie A. Fleming, J.D. jaf@lifeatthebar.com
800.758.6214

Copyright © 2014 Julie A. Fleming, J.D.

ISBN 978-0-9911251-1-1

Printed in the United States of America

Published by: Crow Creek Press Atlanta GA

Designed and typeset by: Razor Edge Press Barnegat NJ

"Fleming has written a definitive guide for lawyers who understand the importance of rainmaking but would prefer to focus their time on performing legal work. Indeed, I think the book goes to the 'reluctant rainmaker' that is in almost all of us to some degree. *The Reluctant Rainmaker* illuminates the connection between practicing law and growing a book of business. With easy-to-apply recommendations for how to get the most benefit from business-building activity, Fleming has offered a guide that every lawyer will be able to use with confidence.

—**John L. North**
Sutherland LLP

"*The Reluctant Rainmaker* is a practical guide for aspiring rainmakers at any stage of a legal career. Through illustrative stories and clear 'how to' directions, Fleming offers a guide that will take the pain out of business development and replace it with success.

—**Don Hutcheson**
Editor and Publisher of *The Complete Lawyer*

"*The Reluctant Rainmaker* will unleash the potential every lawyer has to bring in new business without fear of appearing pushy or desperate."

—**Monica R. Parker, J.D.**
Author of The Unhappy Lawyer: A Roadmap for Finding Meaningful Work Outside of the Law

Dedicated to SHF and JDF

Table of Contents

Foreword to the Second Edition

On February 12, 2009, "Bloody Thursday," U.S. law firms announced layoffs of 800 attorneys and staff, a number that swelled to over 2,000 by month's end and to over 12,000 by the end of the year.

It was that crisis that gave rise to *The Reluctant Rainmaker*. Before the fall of 2008, I had worked with lawyers on a variety of practice-related topics. On a Thursday in late October 2008, I had a full day of appointments scheduled, and by the end of the day each and every client had told me about feared or real layoffs. I quickly realized that I needed to find a solution to help my clients weather the difficulties ahead: without a solution, their practices and my business were at risk.

That solution, of course, was successful business development. I shifted each conversation with my clients to focus on networking with potential clients and referral sources and began to work with them on how to ask for business. My clients worked to raise their profiles and develop their business relationships. The next 18 months were more difficult than my clients or I could have imagined, but all of my clients survived and remained in practice. Some were laid off but were able to find alternative employment, others opted to launch a new firm, and yet others managed to survive the layoffs and to emerge with a deeper understanding and greater skill of the business underlying the practice of law.

I was left with this strong conviction that underlies my client work and breathes life into *The Reluctant Rainmaker*: every successful private practice lawyer is a rainmaker who consistently executes a strategic business development plan and generates a steady pipeline of new business. But lawyers rarely receive any education on how to bring in in new business, and the vast volume of "how to" materials designed to offer that instruction often educate on the details of how to build a book of business without adequately addressing the strategy and mindset required for success. It's the gap that *The Reluctant Rainmaker* seeks to fill.

Although much has changed in the five years since the first edition of *The Reluctant Rainmaker* was published, the basic principles remain the same. To bring in new business, a lawyer must take part in activities that will develop his skill and others' perception of his skill in practice. He must establish and develop relationships with the right people. He must conduct masterful prospective client consultations and ask for business, and he must be comfortable doing so. And once hired, he must deliver excellent client service so his clients will speak highly of him and send their own repeat business (where appropriate) or referrals to him. Rainmaking is really that simple, at least in broad brushstrokes.

Where rainmaking gets complicated, however, is in setting the strategy to accomplish those goals and effectively implementing the tactics that bring the strategy to life. Lawyers must now contend with social media,

Internet marketing, and the rise of new avenues to reach potential clients and referral sources, along with the traditional routes of networking, writing, speaking, teaching, and so on.

The second edition of The Reluctant Rainmaker is designed to identify and explain the traditional routes of building business and to highlight the approaches that are working now.

Introduction

Why did you go to law school? I always enjoy asking lawyers this question, because the answers are varied and almost always interesting. Sometimes family history paves the path to law school, either by design or by desire. The latter was true for me: my father is a lawyer, and I grew up listening to stories about his work and meeting his colleagues. I knew by the time I was in high school that I wanted to be a lawyer. I did consider other professions every now and then, but the law kept drawing me back. And I was fortunate to discover that I loved the law when I finally got into practice. Others I meet have a similar story, except some find that law is not what they hoped it would be, and others even know from the start that it is their family's burning desire for them to be a lawyer, while they would prefer something else.

Lawyers often share an experience that they or someone close to them had that propelled them into law. One woman told me that she had spent hours volunteering in a battered women's shelter, which led her to represent these women, to help protect them and their families. Another shared that he was always intrigued by health care, specifically how drug companies invented and marketed their medicines, and how the public benefited (or not) from those drugs. These stories are rich.

Of course, some lawyers tell me that they had no idea what to do when they moved into their senior year of college, so they went to law school by default. Although these lawyers often have an uphill battle—law is simply too demanding to find job satisfaction in practice without a reason for practicing—many become good lawyers who enjoy their work. Others leave the law, but carry the knowledge and lessons with them into other fields.

Have you noticed it yet, the secret of the reluctant rainmaker? I have never had a single lawyer tell me that he went into law to bring in business. Not one person has told me about the joys of networking, the pleasures of asking for business, or the delights of building a book of business. Make no mistake: clients are often at the heart of a lawyer's reason for being in practice, because lawyers generally do want to help others. But getting the clients and having the work to do is always assumed. It is a shadowy, rarely considered aspect of practice for those who are deciding to be lawyers, and not much more for those in law school.

Nor does law school teach client development. Yes, classes are offered (sometimes) on how to work with clients, and some schools even have a class or two on the business of practicing law. Rainmaking 101 is not, however, offered by any law school as a regular part of the curriculum. The law school approach seems to be: we will teach you how to think like a lawyer and perhaps even how to practice law, but you must figure out elsewhere how to get clients on whom to practice. We could debate for hours whether that is an appropriate policy, and those debates are in fact taking place, but the fact remains: for most lawyers today, law school offered no training in business development.

Given that background, perhaps it is unsurprising how often lawyers say things like, "I didn't go to law school to be a salesperson!" We want to be excellent lawyers, and we want to represent our clients to the best of our ability, but we generally do not feel a zeal for recruiting clients. Fear often steps in, as well. Conscious of the public perception of lawyers and of the explicit ethical boundaries in our profession, lawyers often fear that they will come across as pushy, or obnoxious, or desperate if they ask for business. Anyone who has met a lawyer whose approach focuses on herself, her work, and how she could help you knows that such a tactic is arrogant and unattractive. *No*, many lawyers shudder, *that is not for us*.

Without clients, though, there is no practice. No business. No income. Someone has to be willing to get clients. If a firm has more than a few lawyers, it is possible that one or more rainmakers can lead the crusade, schmoozing their way to client roster success for the firm and bringing in the business to keep the non–rainmaker lawyers afloat. Over recent years, however, those lawyers have realized that they have a skill and a strength that is highly marketable because so many other lawyers lack it. They may demand premium pay, reasoning that no one else would have an income without the rainmaker, and they may be willing to move to another firm when the opportunity presents itself. A firm with just one strong rainmaker will find itself in a tenuous position, and firms that woo rainmakers with large, guaranteed income teeter on the brink of disaster.

Sole practitioners face a similar but perhaps even more dire challenge. If a solo lawyer cannot bring in business, the practice will soon fail. Some larger firm lawyers may have the luxury of relying on others to bring in billable work (or at least they *think* they have that luxury) but sole practitioners do not. What do you call a solo who cannot make rain? Broke. A job seeker. And possibly unemployable.

The reluctant rainmaker is one who understands how important it is to be able to bring in clients… But she does not care for the idea of business development. She may see it as a necessary task, something that is a distasteful part of practicing law. If so, she may struggle to find a way to "do the rainmaking thing," because her dislike for it will keep her from spending time laying plans and executing them effectively. The reluctant rainmaker often takes on a random assortment of activities—writing here, speaking there, networking everywhere—only to discover that random activity produces random results. She might even get results that feel like the start of real success, but she is unlikely to get a sustainable quality or quantity of results, as she might if she could find a way to enjoy the process. She likely feels tremendous pressure (from within herself and externally) to bring in business, and she probably resents having to work so hard at something that is not her goal.

Another reluctant rainmaker may decide that he just does not have the skills necessary to bring in new business. He may give up before trying, or he may plan and study and try to learn all about rainmaking so that he will feel more comfortable with the process. These would-be rainmakers are slow to take action, and their steps are rarely coordinated into a consistent overall approach. This type of reluctant rainmaker may have a flawless plan on paper, but he will probably try an activity once or twice, conclude it does not work for him, and move on to another, never realizing that consistent activity is required to yield results.

Yet other reluctant rainmakers are willing to try their hands at business development, but are at a loss where to start. This aspiring rainmaker sees so many components to client development that she feels overwhelmed and unsure where to begin. Focusing on the fact that she does not yet know everything about business development and thus hesitating for fear of making a misstep, she remains unaware of where her rainmaking strengths lie.

This book is written for the reluctant rainmaker. Inside, you will find the background information that will help you to understand why business development is so critical, and you will discover a step–by–step guide as you explore the rainmaker's toolkit. You will create your own cohesive business development plan, which will provide the clear direction you need to take action. You may not become a rainmaker extraordinaire, and you may not come to love the process. You will, however, learn to build a solid book of business that will support you in developing a successful, satisfying, and sustainable practice.

I recommend that you skim through the parts of this book that are most interesting to you first. If you consider yourself to be an introvert and wonder how you can be successful in rainmaking, go straight to that chapter. After you have satisfied your curiosity, read the book from beginning to end, with sticky notes and a pen and paper or a computer nearby. Use the book: underline, write in it, turn down corners of pages, and take notes, especially when something I say generates an idea. When you reach Chapter 3, go through the exercises and create your business development plan in writing. Throughout the book, you will see references to additional resources on the website for *The Reluctant Rainmaker*. Use the forms, and study and model the templates. They will make the process easier for you.

You must engage with this material if your goal is to benefit from reading it. If you simply skim through, close the book, and put it on the shelf, you will have wasted your time. If, however, you work through the book, develop your plan, follow your plan, and accept the suggestions for getting additional help and support with your business development activities, you will succeed. Make a clear decision: work the book and keep going until you reach the goals you set, or close it now.

Be sure to download the resources available at TheReluctantRainmaker.com. These resources (which are referenced throughout the book) will guide you in your business development planning and the execution of your plan.

A word about client stories included

Because client confidentiality is paramount in all coaching engagements, the stories included herein represent composite clients, with names and other identifying details changed.

PART I

Foundations of Legal Marketing

Chapter 1

Basic Premises of Business Development

Before setting off on your journey to becoming a rainmaker, it is helpful to pause and look into a few basic premises that underlie everything you will do to bring in new business. Jumping off into the questions of what you should do, when, and how is important, but unless your rainmaking efforts are well-grounded, chances are you will lose motivation, base your plans on a fundamental misconception, or otherwise misstep as you get started.

Legal Skill Is Not Enough

Since you are reading this book, you likely already understand that technical legal skill is not enough in today's economy. Proficiency in practicing law is little more than a minimum requirement and, for a great many clients, not much of a distinguishing characteristic. (Your reputation as a superstar lawyer can set you apart from others in your area of practice, but reputation and actual expertise are not always the same thing.) Make no mistake: a lawyer's or law firm's reputation and perceived legal expertise will be increasingly critical as the matter at stake increases in importance. Few clients who have an option would hire "just any lawyer" for bet–the–company litigation. Those matters are, however, relatively unusual. In more ordinary matters, perhaps a few clients (mostly lawyers themselves or those who practiced law before moving into another field) may be able to judge an adequate brief from one that is excellent, but most will recognize only competency. Even if you are a legal genius, able to produce work product that would make [insert your legal idol here] weep with pride, you must have clients upon whom to visit your extraordinary skill.

If you imagine that you can sit in your office and crank out your work product, allowing others to bring in the clients who will benefit from your expertise, please reconsider. In 2009 and 2010, thousands of talented lawyers were laid off from large firms, were stunned to find that their firms dissolved from underneath them, or discovered that despite their best efforts, they did not have sufficient work to keep a sole practice afloat. While the pace of those practice failures has slowed dramatically, layoffs continue and practices still end due to a lack of clients. Many factors culminate in each of those unhappy situations, but the common thread is quite simple: an insufficient client base.

Lawyers who know how to bring in clients succeed in practice.

Lawyers who can bring in new business have more professional security and options than those who cannot.

Larger firm lawyers who are able to land new clients and new matters are unlikely to be laid off: doing so would be against a firm's economic interest. Likewise, you might discover that your firm has failed, but chances are good that you would have an easy lateral move before or after the failure. For sole practitioners, rainmaking ability is probably the single most critical skill in launching and maintaining your practice.

Those who do not bring in new business and new clients (and who choose not to learn) may succeed in good economic times, but they are quickly cast aside when the economy becomes difficult, and they typically have trouble finding a new job without any ability to bring in business to support themselves. The arrogance of expecting that legal skill alone will be sufficient to build a lasting practice is too often followed by the anguish of discovering that skill is not enough. Regardless of the size of your firm, you are secure in your practice only to the extent that you can bring in clients to fill it. Lawyers who know how to bring in clients succeed in practice.

One reason that rainmakers succeed in practice is because they deliver more value to their clients than those who simply do the billable work entrusted to them. Many business development activities—writing substantive articles, making presentations at CLE meetings or industry groups, for example—require rainmakers to be up–to–date on the latest developments in their field. As a result, these activities enhance rainmakers' expertise as well as others' perception of their expertise. Moreover, because rainmakers tend to build relationships with their clients and contacts, they are also better positioned to bring new information to these clients and to be more proactive in helping clients respond to the information. While clients do not necessarily associate these advantages with their lawyers' rainmaking activities, it is clear that the business development activities go hand-in-hand with client benefit.

Have you heard the old saw that held that law firms need four categories of lawyers: finders, minders, grinders, and binders?

It is still true to some degree, though today's atmosphere requires lawyers to develop their skills in all of these areas, rather than simply selecting the most comfortable skill set and roosting there. ***Finders*** are those who find the work, better known today as rainmakers. ***Minders*** are those who perform administrative tasks and coordinate the efforts of the finders, grinders, and binders to be sure that the firm will run as a cohesive whole; examples include managing partners, the executive committee, and team leaders. ***Grinders*** are those who grind out the client work, and ***binders*** are those who bring the members of a firm together by (for example) inviting a small group to lunch or recognizing achievements of the firm's lawyers.

Because rainmakers succeed in practice, they tend to enjoy more influence and higher compensation than their non-rainmaker peers. Why? Because those whose skills are limited to doing the work are easily replaced. Adequate lawyers are, especially in a difficult economy, plentiful and eager to work. Losing a "grinder" may slow down a representation, since any departing lawyer will likely take knowledge of her clients and matters, leaving a vacuum of knowledge that must be filled by a replacement. That vacuum can be filled easily under all but the most unusual circumstances, and the grinder's departure will be little more than a quick bump in the road. Losing a "finder," however, means a loss of business that lawyer would have delivered, and it probably means the loss of at least some of the clients the finder was responsible for landing. No firm wants to see clients going elsewhere, so a finder is much less replaceable, and the rainmaker is encouraged to stay by being accorded more influence in the firm and more money. If you want to be so valuable that you are effectively irreplaceable to your firm, you must be a rainmaker.

Rainmakers also have higher levels of professional satisfaction than those who simply do whatever work is assigned to them. Why? The process of bringing in new clients and new matters requires a lawyer to develop business relationships with someone—a current client, someone the lawyer knew in law school, even someone with whom the lawyer has a purely social relationship—and the business that results very often comes through a client with whom the lawyer likes to work. Thanks to the same process, the rainmaker will also be able to decide which cases to accept. He will most likely accept matters in the field of interest that he finds intellectually stimulating, challenging, meaningful, or enjoyable. Is this always true? No, of course not: rainmakers may take on routine matters that are not so exciting, but the great likelihood is that the rainmaker will assign those cases to another lawyer. By being able to pick

Being a rainmaker creates high levels of professional satisfaction.

and choose (to a large degree, at least) which cases to work on, the rainmaker creates high levels of professional satisfaction.

Finally, for non-solo lawyers, partnership decisions tend to rely on some demonstration of rainmaking ability. Although some firms do not require an associate to be a rainmaker at the time of election, it is unlikely that a firm would welcome a new partner without believing that she is capable of bringing in business to help support the firm's growth. Equity partners are almost always rainmakers, for the simple reason that most partnerships would be loathe to share the firm's profits with a lawyer who had no hand in recruiting the clients that yielded the profits—back to the greater influence enjoyed by rainmakers.

You may be wondering whether you need to become a superstar rainmaker to enjoy the advantages outlined here. Not necessarily. Bringing in a single small matter will not net the same benefits that a rainmaker extraordinaire will experience, but the increased opportunities that flow from increased rainmaking are represented on something like a sliding scale. Not everyone can be (or wants to be) a master rainmaker, but everyone can learn to develop the skills necessary to bring in *some* new work. The more consistently and strategically you engage in the processes that tend to yield new business, the better your results are likely to be and the more benefits will likely flow your way.

Rainmaking Is Not About Selling

One objection that lawyers commonly make when approaching business development is that they want to be legal professionals, not sales professionals. Most reluctant rainmakers dread anything that looks or feels like sales, and painting the process of business development with a sales brush is the kiss of death for many lawyers. But here is the good news: rainmaking is not about selling.

Selling is typically the process (to skeptical lawyers, at least) of convincing unsuspecting buyers that they need to purchase something. It is creating demand for a product or service, or creating demand for a specific purveyor of a product or service. Although most everyone enjoys buying things and services on a regular basis, most people dislike being sold to, which in turn creates resistance to selling. Throw in many lawyers' concept of the practice of law as more of a profession and less of a business (a view that seems somewhat anachronistic today, though to the delight of those who still see the law as a calling or profession and not merely a vocation, it lingers) and it is easy to see why some lawyers reject anything that looks or feels like a sales pitch.

> ***The best time to begin business development activity is several years ago; the next best time to begin is now.***

Most lawyers are able to identify how their work benefits their clients, whether that work is handling a nitpicky tax issue for a multi–national corporation or a custody dispute for a father who feels that he is losing valuable time with his children. Rainmaking, however, may make a lawyer feel like the stereotypical used car salesman foisting his services on an uninterested public. When I work with clients whose sales repulsion is blocking their business development success, I suggest a simple perspective shift. One–on–one client development is the process of finding a match between lawyer, matter, and client. Instead of casting that process as sales, why not cast it as an opportunity to offer help to a client who will benefit?

Engaging in a discussion designed to reveal the potential client's needs and to determine whether that lawyer is a good match for those needs and the client's personality is not selling to the client. It is a conversation, a mutual exploration, an offer to guide that client through the legal situation confronting her. The conversation may be quick or protracted, but at its base, it is intended to match the lawyer's skill to the client's needs, in service to the client. Without the need, there is no representation. The "courting," in which lawyer and client are both deciding whether there is a match, is a give-and-take process, not something that is done *by* the lawyer *to* the potential client. And that is what rainmaking is: a conversation–based process of finding new business.

Strategy and Consistency

Rainmaking is not just *any* conversation, though: it is a strategic conversation, designed with a particular purpose in mind, that results from consistent cultivation of relationships. Strategy is a key component of business development because setting out without a plan rarely succeeds. Each lawyer will have a different approach to growing his practice. All thriving rainmakers, however, have at least one trait in common: consistency in rainmaking activity. As Jay Conrad Levinson, author of the *Guerilla Marketing* series of books, wrote, "a mediocre marketing program with [consistency] will always prove more profitable than a brilliant marketing program without [consistency]."

Why does consistency matter? Suppose you are researching an area of law to get a feel for it, knowing that you are going to need to affiliate with an expert in the area. Would you be likely to contact someone who keeps popping up as an author of articles that address your topic and who has also spoken on the issue at a number of CLE meetings? Would you be more or less likely to contact someone whose name comes up once as an author, or once as a speaker, or perhaps once as a member of a relevant committee? Most of us would be more eager to speak with the first lawyer, expecting that she has developed greater expertise in the area through consistent efforts in writing and speaking on the topic. The same selection and expectations would likely hold for a client searching for a lawyer. (And a lawyer who cannot be found cannot be hired, so being visible is central to success in practice.)

Strategy + Consistency = Rainmaking Success

Commitment and consistency in business development activities pays off because it increases the depth of your experience and credentials in a particular area, and it creates multiple impressions of you as someone knowledgeable in a certain area of the law. Whether it is writing, as in the example above, or in performing *pro bono* work, undertaking some client development activity once is unlikely to make a significant impact. But if you repeat that activity regularly, making it a routine part of your schedule, you will begin to gain some traction, to know people in the relevant area and to be known, and potentially to acquire a reputation as an expert. Sustained effort yields results.

When my clients ask me for recommendations on

consistency in business development, I recommend that they use one of the following approaches:

- **Daily activity:** Complete one business development task every single day. These tasks can vary between quick and easy (making a phone call to check in with a client or referral source) to protracted and challenging (setting aside four hours to work on an article related to your practice area). The benefit of daily activity is that you chip away at your task list, and missing a single day does little to compromise your progress.

- **Weekly activity:** Set aside certain blocks of time each week to ensure that you continue moving forward in your business development plan. If you take this approach, I recommend that you set a minimum weekly goal of two hours devoted to rainmaking activity. Beware slippage if you decide to use weekly activity, however: while missing a single day's implementation of your plan will create only a negligible slowdown, missing a full week of activity can cause your progress to grind to a halt.

- **Annual activity:** In Part II of this book, you will find specific recommendations relating to the hours that lawyers in various levels of seniority should expect to spend on business development each year. I strongly recommend that you divide these hours into daily or weekly hours and track them accordingly. An annual push for business will not yield the same results that a consistent flow of activity will.

- **Task–based activity:** If you prefer to operate based

on tasks rather than on time, choose three tactics (discussed infra) from your business development plan and make sure that you implement each of them monthly. You must, however, be sure that your activities are larger in scope if task–based than if time–based. For example, you might select networking at a certain meeting and following up with three people as one of your tasks to be completed in a month.

Decide which approach to ensuring consistency works best with your schedule, your personal preferences, and your business development plan. Just remember this key formula: Strategy + Consistency = Rainmaking Success.

Why Would–Be Rainmakers Fail

Business development ability is a learned skill, not an inherited trait. Some attitudes and tendencies, however, tend to undermine lawyers' rainmaking goals. We have already discussed failure to implement your business development activities on a consistent basis, which is probably the most common mistake I see lawyers making. It is not, however, the only mistake. Notice whether you recognize any of these errors in your own thinking and behavior.

- **Failure to plan before executing.** Some lawyers strike out into rainmaker activity without first creating a plan to direct their actions. This approach almost guarantees disappointment and burnout.

Eric, a fifth–year litigator in a large firm, decided

it was time to begin his rainmaking efforts. He had attended a business development seminar hosted by his firm for its associates, and he remembered the speaker's comment that writing can be a good tactic for business development. He had just finished working on a brief that focused on some thorny issues of the attorney-client privilege, so he began writing an article summarizing his research and offering recommendations to avoid waiving the privilege. When he had polished the article, having invested about 15 hours into the project, he then searched for journals to which he could submit it.

If you allow yourself to become easily discouraged, you will rarely see the results of your effort.

To his surprise and disappointment, the article seemed to be wrong for just about every publication he contacted—too long, not practical enough, not academic enough, and so on. Fortunately, with some significant rewriting, Eric was able to place the article in his state bar's Young Lawyers Division newsletter. Unfortunately, since Eric's practice area was securities litigation and most financial industry clients are represented by seasoned attorneys (not young lawyers), his effort did little to build his credibility or to appeal to his target clients. While the additional line on his resume was beneficial, was it worth the nearly 20 hours of effort? Uncertain, Eric decided that writing was not such a good way to land clients after all. If he had made a plan before he began writing, however, Eric might have identified the publications in which he would like to place his article, and he might have discussed the proposed scope of the article with editors to gauge their interest. By taking those preparatory steps, Eric could have adjusted his article to meet the publishers' needs, or he could have decided before investing 20 hours that he was unlikely to realize a benefit sufficient to justify that expenditure of time.

- **Failure to persist.** Occasionally you will strike business development gold, such as quickly turning a new acquaintance into a client or landing a new client in response to an article you wrote or a presentation you made. Much more often, however, you will find that rainmaking is a process that culminates in new business in only a small percentage of instances. It is not a "quick fix;" it requires a willingness to stick with the process. When Beth called me to explore business development coaching, I asked her a few questions about what was and was not going well in her practice and, specifically, in her rainmaking efforts. Beth told me that she had tried a lot of approaches, none of which had worked well, so she needed to find something uniquely suited to her. When I inquired what she had done in the past, she reeled off a variety of activities, including networking. I asked her to describe her networking attempts, and she listed six or seven groups she had visited, all of which were well suited for her practice.

My next question revealed the problem: Beth had visited most of the groups only once, and none more than twice. As you will learn in Chapter 12, networking requires consistent attendance because some time is required to start making connections with a group. Certainly not all of the groups Beth had visited would be appropriate for her goals, but a single visit almost never yields sufficient information to judge how effective a group might be as a networking forum. Beth and I worked together over a period of several months, during which time she honed in on two groups, attending them regularly, connecting with people and getting to know them, and ultimately generating business. The difference? Persistence.

- **"I don't have time!"** Except in difficult economic circumstances, lawyers very rarely have hours of spare time just waiting to be filled. Chapter 5 offers specific tactics to maximize your time for business development activities, but to be successful you must adopt the mindset that you can integrate your business development activities into your day–to–day professional hours and your personal life. The more you enjoy the activities you pursue, the more willing you will be to devote time to them. If you hate golf, I would not recommend you pursue it as a client development tactic even though it is the quintessential example. Instead, maybe you and some of your clients would enjoy attending a concert, a cooking class, or a wine tasting. Choose what you enjoy and you will be much happier devoting extra hours to that activity.
- **"But it's easier for *them*."** Lawyers who have not yet found their rainmaking stride often tell me how much easier business development is for others.

Men tell me it is easier for women, and vice versa. Small firm lawyers tell me it is easier in large firms (and vice versa), and sole practitioners tell me that small and large firm lawyers have all the advantages. The truth is that, while some lawyers do enjoy special advantages—those who really enjoy networking, for instance, or those who benefit from the reputation of their well-known and highly respected families—business development is merely different for those lawyers, not necessarily easier.

- **"I'm too new to bring in business."** Newer lawyers know that their first priority is learning the law and the skills required for practice. However, junior lawyers have opportunities to maintain relationships with former classmates (law school and undergraduate) and to forge relationships with peers at client organizations. Junior lawyers in law firms also have more experienced colleagues with expertise and reputations that may interest potential clients and contacts. Do not let your status as a new lawyer stop you from doing what you can do now and learning what you can do as you advance. (Chapter 17 offers suggestions especially for you.)

- **Unrealistic expectations, leading to disappointment.** Especially when every law practice management periodical seems to offer business development guidance, some lawyers expect that implementing a few activities should be enough to have clients flood into their practice. One such lawyer was Harry, a patent attorney who wrote three articles for a foreign language newspaper and brought in two new clients as a result. When he reported his results, Harry was distressed that his results were so paltry and told me that he planned to quit. When I informed him that he was experiencing surprisingly good results from his writing, he decided to continue, and after a few months he had a consistent business pipeline that was directly attributable to those articles. Harry's unrealistic expectations that each article should generate its own flood of business nearly undermined that success.

If you recognize that you are experiencing any of these obstacles, you can choose differently from now on. You will find ideas and suggestions in subsequent chapters to help you adjust your outlook and your approach to business development. As you proceed, though, watch for these obstacles to crop up. Simply knowing how common they are may help you to see an excuse for what it is. The best time to begin business development activity is several years ago; the next best time to begin is *now.*

Get Support for Your Efforts

The best thing you can do to recognize these obstacles for what they are is to affiliate yourself with others who are working on their own rainmaking efforts. Reading books and attending seminars is useful because you will learn basic approaches and perhaps how to modify them to meet your specific needs. But nothing can match the effectiveness of supplementing that education with support from someone who is able to help you tailor what you have learned to your community, your practice, your personality, and more. You can find or create a variety of opportunities to get this kind of specialized attention.

The first, and perhaps the easiest, opportunity is working with a mentor. Find someone who is an established rainmaker (this is not a place for the blind to be leading the blind!) and whom you respect and like. The best mentoring opportunities happen organically, when conversations begin to build on one another and before you know it, you are working with someone who is a real mentor, not someone who has been assigned to you. However, you can recruit a mentor through a more organized search by identifying good candidates, talking with them enough to discover whether your personalities and interests mesh sufficiently, and if so, asking them to mentor you.

While a full discussion of mentoring is outside the scope of this book, a few points are critical. The responsibility for the relationship rests primarily on the lawyer being mentored. When someone has agreed to mentor you, however formal or informal the relationship may be, it is your responsibility to request meetings, to ask questions to deepen your learning, and to seek the feedback that you need. Do not make the mistake, though, of believing that mentoring is a one–way relationship. Ideally, a mentor should benefit as much as the lawyer he is mentoring. Perhaps you can bring new perspectives, new technology, or fresh approaches to the mentor's work. The richest mentoring relationships, and the ones that last the longest, benefit

The richest mentoring relationships, and the ones that last the longest, benefit both parties.

both parties. Also consider that you can, and perhaps should, have more than one mentor.

Another option for getting support is to work with a rainmaker group. Meeting regularly with trusted colleagues creates a forum for accountability, venting, and seeking feedback on challenges. Building strong connections with reliable confidants offers an antidote to what may seem like a never–ending stream of bad news and can create ripples of opportunity as information is shared. These professional relationships pay huge dividends professionally and personally.

If you are looking to grow your practice, joining a rainmaker group will create a healthy competition (who wants to be the only member who failed to complete action steps as promised?) and will give you a forum for feedback on your business development progress that you are unlikely to receive otherwise. More than just support, group meetings with lawyers in whose judgment you have confidence can yield remarkable progress as you benefit from your cohort's feedback and suggestions.

How can you get involved with one of these groups? One option is to create your own group by inviting a few trusted friends and colleagues to join you in a discussion group. I recommend that you limit the size to no more than ten lawyers and that you set a six–month commitment. Meet at least twice per month, and assign the leadership role to each member on a rotating basis. The leader will be responsible for running the meeting, for making sure that the conversation remains relevant to the group's purpose, and for introducing new resources.

While such self–selected groups can be effective, very often they dissolve when other commitments take precedence because there is no "skin in the game" beyond the agreement to work in the group. Their structure may crumble without someone who has been granted leadership authority by the group. As a result, many lawyers prefer to join professionally–operated groups. Coaches, consultants, and recruiters offer these groups (often described as "Mastermind Groups") to a limited number of participants. The organizer is responsible for attracting the group members, for leading the group discussions, for ensuring that group members uphold their commitment to the group, and for offering professional feedback to the members' concerns.

Many groups also feature one–on–one time with the organizer, in which members can get objective feedback and coaching on their opportunities and obstacles. To locate a Mastermind Group, ask colleagues for recommendations, check with coaches or recruiters you know, or run a Google search on "attorney mastermind group" or "lawyer mastermind program."

You will advance much more quickly if you get support in your business development activity. Find a mentor, create a rainmaker group, join a professionally–organized rainmaker mentoring and mastermind group, or hire a coach to work with you one–on–one. Whatever you choose to do, do not rely solely on education. As is true for most aspects of practice, knowledge is good but by itself insufficient to help you meet your business development goals most efficiently.

The Bottom Line for Reluctant Rainmakers

Being a rainmaker affords benefits that will touch every area of your practice, from the most basic—your ability to remain in practice—to the more advanced, such as the enjoyment you find in your practice. Begin working on your business development training and education immediately, and recognize that everyone faces challenges in developing the skills required. Find the support that will help you to set goals, overcome obstacles, and craft strong approaches to client development opportunities. Above all, be strategic and consistent in your activity. By arming yourself with training and support, and by recognizing the common mistakes that trip up aspiring rainmakers, you can lay the foundation for success.

Chapter 2

Business Development Priorities

Because time, energy, and money are limited, identifying priorities and acting accordingly is one of the most important steps for success in any field. A lawyer who focuses on the wrong tasks (concentrating on setting up a flawless filing system, for instance, rather than concentrating on client work product) will fail in practice. Likewise, an aspiring rainmaker who devotes time and energy to the wrong tasks will fail to bring in the desired results. Correct priority identification is particularly critical for reluctant rainmakers because missteps may seem more overpowering to those who would prefer not to engage in business development. Experiencing false starts or disappointing results may dissuade a skeptical or pessimistic would–be rainmaker from continuing with efforts that otherwise might succeed if given sufficient time. Set your priorities appropriately and adapt your activity accordingly.

Rainmaking is about relationships.

Relationships

Rainmaking is about relationships. Some clients will perform an online search to locate a lawyer, and others may place a call based solely on advertising. However, most would–be clients will seek one or more referrals before hiring a lawyer. It is easy to understand why: with approximately 1.1 million lawyers in the United States, and with public skepticism of lawyers always high, clients want some recommendation for a lawyer's skill and service before making a potentially expensive decision. Both individual and corporate clients will likely ask colleagues, business associates, and friends for a referral.

"All things being equal, people will do business with—and refer business to—those people they know, like and trust." This quote, from Bob Burg's excellent book *Endless Referrals,* sums up why relationships serve as the basis for rainmaking. It also clarifies what your priorities should be for business development. Focus first on those who already know, like, and trust you, and then seek to expand those sources of business. That order of approach dictates, in turn, the priorities that you should set as you work to develop your clientele.

Priority #1: Current Clients

Your current clients are your "low hanging fruit." They have hired you at least once, they know intimately how well you serve your clients, and they are uniquely positioned to give an insider's point of view on what it is like to be your client. Accordingly, whether you are seeking repeat engagements or referrals, your current clients are best situated to deliver business to you or to divert it elsewhere. Part II, *infra,* describes a variety of tactics you might use to stay in touch with current clients, but your top priority should be providing excellent client service.

Clients want lawyers who understand and put the client's goals first.

You must pay attention to the substantive part of your representations, of course. Clients may or may not be able to evaluate the technical aspects of your work, but they know whether they got the result they were seeking or, if not, whether they rightly or wrongly ascribe the failure to your skill. In many instances, however, the day–to–day working relationship—how you provide the legal services you offer, in other words—will take center stage in the client's evaluation of your abilities.

Listen to Your Clients

Depending on your area of practice, the matter you undertake for a client may represent the only contact (or one of few) that your client has had with a lawyer. In such an instance, that matter is likely to be an area of primary focus to the client. Your client will want to know in return that, although he is not your only client, you understand how important the matter is to him. Even if you are representing a large corporation in one of many pending matters, you can rest assured that the corporate representatives attach importance to the matter and want to know that you do the same. Matters that are routine to you are unlikely to be equally routine to your clients.

Implicit here is that clients want lawyers who appreciate the client's aim, communicate that they do understand, and convey how the progress or outcome of a matter affects the ultimate goals. Clients want lawyers who understand and place the client's goals first. To accomplish this, you must listen carefully to a client's description of the matter, her goals, and the impact of the matter on other aspects of the client's business or life.

One complaint that clients often have is that some lawyers take on the role of the expert too quickly, offering solutions before fully appreciating the problem or the desired outcome. You will be most effective in offering assistance if you first ask questions and then listen carefully to the answers you receive. Listening telegraphs that you respect the speaker and want the information he is conveying, and it creates the impression that you are seeking to understand what your conversational partner needs. Only when you fully understand can you offer a complete solution to those needs. And by ensuring that you understand before you speak, you will distinguish yourself from other lawyers without even opening your mouth.

Skillful listeners know the three levels of listening and how (and when) to access each. Most of us spend the majority of our time in Level I listening. In Level I, we hear what is said and listen through a filter of, "What does this mean for me?" If you have ever had a conversation in which you are sharing an experience and your partner keeps responding by sharing an analogous experience (or if she responds to every story by "one upping" it to tell an even more notable story about herself), you've experienced Level I. When talking with someone who is listening at Level I, a speaker may feel that the listener is not really listening at all, only hearing the words enough to decide how to respond to them. Talking to someone who is listening at Level I can be deeply frustrating, and a Level I listener will almost certainly miss important information while composing her own response to what is being said.

Level II listening occurs when the listener is focused entirely on the speaker and is working to understand what the information being communicated means for the speaker. Level II is other–focused, and it conveys a deep respect for the speaker and a desire to see what the speaker sees. Listeners engaged at this level are working to put the speaker's words together to understand the full scope of the situation from the speaker's perspective. Skillful lawyers spend most of their conversation time with clients and potential clients engaged at Level II, weighing every word to grasp the speaker's full meaning.

In Level III listening, the listener pays attention not just to the speaker's words but also to her tone of voice, the speed of her speech, her word choice, her body language, and other non–verbal modes of communication. A Level III listener focuses attention on what is being said and how it is being said. Level III is the deepest level of listening, and operating at that level affords the lawyer access to tremendous amounts of information that he can then use to craft a response that will meet the speaker's concerns. The skill of Level III listening is not easily acquired, but the investment of energy and focus pays significant returns.

> ***A Level III listener focuses attention on what is being said and how it is being said.***

A lawyer who listens primarily on Level III will gain a full understanding of a situation and, as a result, will be able to craft a solution that truly meets the needs expressed. Listening on this level and delivering results that exceed the client's expectations will, over time, help the lawyer to move to "trusted advisor" status, in which the client trusts the lawyer to hold the client's interest paramount throughout the representation. At trusted advisor status, the lawyer becomes (to some degree) a partner in the client's business or life, someone to whom the client feels comfortable turning for advice and help and to whom the client will be eager to refer others, confident in the knowledge you will represent them equally well.

Listening well will pay remarkable dividends. Good listening distinguishes you from those who seek to provide their solution without a full appreciation of the situation. You will also convey the impression that you are thorough and attentive. Similarly, applying deep listening skills to your current clients will help you to pick up information that will allow you to represent the client effectively, and will demonstrate to your client that you consider his matter worthy of your full attention.

Communicate Well

One of the top complaints clients have about their lawyers is the failure to communicate. Clients want lawyers who communicate proactively regarding the progress in their matter, who share new developments that may affect strategy or outcome, and who avoid having the client experience any surprises in the course of the representation. One way to ensure that your clients receive the amount and kind of communication that they want is to discuss it with them at the beginning of the engagement. Questions such as these will help you to set your communications plan with each client:

- How would you like me to communicate with you: telephone, e-mail, or regular mail?
- How often would you like me to give you an update on the progress of your matter? What kind of report would you prefer? (Examples include oral reports and formal or informal written reports.) Should anyone else be copied?
- Would you like to see substantive correspondence and legal documents before we file them? If so, how would you like us to send those documents to you?
- Would you like copies of all correspondence we receive? If so, how would you like us to send those documents to you?
- Are there any regularly scheduled meetings for which we should prepare an update, such as a meeting of the Board of Directors?
- What else should we know to be certain that you get the information you need when and how you need it?

These questions, and others that will flow as follow–up in the course of your conversation, will help ensure that you communicate with your clients on the schedule and in the way they prefer.

Unless a client specifies that she wants very little communication, you might consider implementing a policy that you will reach out to each client by telephone or provide a written update via e-mail on a regular schedule, perhaps once or twice a month. Lawyers know that progress sometimes slows down for reasons outside our control—another lawyer's leave of absence, a court's delayed ruling on a motion that serves as a decision point for future strategy, and so on. Clients, however, may not understand those delays or may ascribe them to your inattention. By checking in with each client on a regular basis, you make certain that the client understands exactly what is happening with the matter and knows what to expect in terms of next steps.

Be Responsive

You should also discuss the amount of time in which your clients can expect to have a response from you when they contact you to inquire about their matter. No reasonable client expects his lawyer to be on call at all times, but establishing your usual operating procedure upfront manages your clients' expectations. For example, you might let clients know that you will return telephone calls within four hours and respond to e-mails within one business day. When you share such a policy, however, you must abide by it. One of the surest routes to dissatisfied clients is to set expectations and then fail to meet them.

> *Managing expectation is critical.*

Consider introducing your clients (at least by telephone or information packet, if not in person) to your assistant and any other lawyers who will be working on the client's matter. By doing so, you show your clients that your assistant and other lawyers are integral parts of the team, which will likely make them more receptive to the option of talking with other office personnel when you are unavailable. Depending on your clients and your area of practice, you even might consider providing certain clients with your home or cell telephone numbers.

Finally, create a system to manage expectations when you are out of the office. We all know from experience how frustrating it is to leave a voicemail or to send an e-mail, not realizing that the recipient is out of the office. Clients experience the same frustration, and most clients will not distinguish between frustration born of the willful failure to respond (when you are in the office but "too busy" to respond, a dangerous message to convey too often) and that resulting from failure to respond because you are not in the office and have not yet received the message. Managing expectation is critical.

An easy solution is to add an "out of office" message to your voicemail and e-mail if you expect to be away, stating the date or dates on which you will be absent (or in meetings that will keep you fully occupied) and when you expect to respond to voicemails or e-mails received during that time. Alternatively, if you have an assistant you trust, you might have him check and respond to important e-mails and voicemails, letting those who contact you know when they will hear directly from you. You could also designate someone to handle communications that do not require your input while you are away, or you might forward your telephone and emails to a smartphone. How you choose to manage expectations matters less than the simple fact that you do arrange a method to manage clients' expectations.

Share Bad News Appropriately

In almost every project, something will occur that will displease the client. Even if the problem arises from circumstances that have nothing to do with you, how you share news about a problem with your client may significantly impact how she perceives working with you. Delivering bad news is one of the most challenging communications issues that lawyers face, but planning can make the conversation as productive as possible while minimizing the negative impact on the attorney/client relationship. Be sure to deliver the news as soon as possible. Bad news does not improve with age, and your client may lose confidence in you if she gets a whiff of the news from another source.

To begin a conversation about a problem, let your client know you have something to discuss and ask for the amount of time you expect the conversation to require. In other words, do not call and let the news dribble out while your client is checking his watch and needing to get to another meeting. Provide any necessary background at the beginning. For instance, "Stan, you probably remember that we filed a motion to compel a few weeks ago so we can get documents about XYZ Corp.'s finances." If there's any confusion about the background, explain. And then spit out the news you need to convey. "Stan, the judge has ruled against us."

> ***Do not try to avoid sharing bad news with a client.***

Explaining what the news means is, of course, the crux of the conversation. Two things may happen after you tell the client what has occurred, depending on the magnitude of the news: either the client will be silent and wait for you to explain, or she may be angry. Unless you (or the firm) made a mistake, do not apologize. Do empathize and, where appropriate, describe what went wrong or what factors yielded this result. If a solution is needed, or if logical next steps exist, explain what they are and advise the client on what you recommend. Be sure you have thought through your proposal. You will lose credit for any "solution" you put forward that may create additional problems unless you can explain a credible risk/reward balance for your proposed approach.

Do not try to avoid sharing bad news with your client. Unless you can solve the problem (and almost without exception, even if you can) your client deserves to know what has happened. This is an integrity issue; it also guards your reputation. Failure to share necessary news will destroy your client's trust in you. On the other hand, when you explain negative developments and offer suggestions on how to handle them effectively, you have an opportunity to increase your client's confidence.

Be Reliable with Cost Estimates and Billing

All clients want to have some reasonable estimate of how much a project will cost. When you provide such an estimate, consider letting the client know what factors could change your estimate. For example, if you provide an estimate to deliver a demand letter for a past–due payment, you might also estimate the additional cost if you are required to draft a complaint, as well as if you move into litigation and the case settles on summary judgment after discovery is completed or if it goes to trial.

Each estimate should be tailored to the client's needs—if, for instance, the client in the previous example tells you that for cost or business reasons he will not take a dispute to trial under any circumstances, you probably should not provide an estimate for going to trial. If you had reason to think that the information would be useful, you might provide the estimate couched in language reflecting your understanding that current circumstances suggest that trial is not currently a viable option.

When you have provided a cost estimate, be sure to update your client immediately if anything occurs to change that estimate materially. You might even tell new clients that you seek to manage fees in accord with your estimate and ask what variances would need their approval. By initiating this conversation, you demonstrate the importance that you place on your clients' preferences and also ensure that you do not fail to mention a fee variance that seems minor to you, only to discover that the increase is substantial to your client.

No client enjoys paying for legal services, and most are concerned that lawyers' fees are too high or hours too loosely billed. If viewed properly, your invoice can function as a substitute for a conversation in which lawyer and client sit down, review what has been done in the last month or so, and total up the hours accumulated. (This discussion assumes, of course, that a matter is being handled on an hourly basis. The same kinds of records should be kept for all matters, even if not shared with the client.) Using that framework, what do you want your clients to find when they read your bills? What you do not want is clear:

- You do not want them to wonder how much time you/your firm spent on a matter;

- You do not want them to wonder who did the work;
- You do not want them to wonder what each member of the team did on their case;
- You do not want them to wonder why a new name has suddenly shown up on an invoice;
- You do not want them to wonder why it is necessary to have so many internal meetings, whether they are really effective, or why each member has listed a different amount of time for the same meeting (assuming that your client is one of the diminishing number willing to pay for internal meetings);
- You do not want them to wonder whether work is being duplicated or whether a matter has too many lawyers working on it; and
- You do not want them to wonder if the work you are doing is really worth it.

It is standard to require attorneys and paralegals to keep timesheets that describe in detail the work they have performed. The issue, though, is how well that standard is honored. As you are filling out your daily timesheet, consider the information value of your billing. Block billing is easy to do, but very difficult for clients to interpret. An entry such as, "2.5 hours, reviewed documents and

Draft your timesheets so that your clients know who did what, why, and when.

drafted/revised motion to compel" will leave a client wondering how long each task required. She will be even less pleased if she finds an entry the next day for more time on the motion to compel if she assumes that the 2.5 hours covered the entire motion when in fact you merely reviewed documents and drafted the motion but not the memorandum in support. Block billing creates questions. Instead, consider whether you should indicate more precisely the amount of time you spent on each task, or whether it would be preferable to include multiple entries.

Although it is essential to remember that your bills may be discoverable and that they must not include privileged information, consider how you may communicate the scope of your work without crossing the line. For instance, you might include entries like, "Researched law re admissibility of [opposing party's] statement in [brief] that [whatever]."

Draft your timesheets so that your clients know who did what, why, and when. When you review invoices, check for incomplete descriptions, inconsistencies, and any information that might be confusing or disturbing to your client. While your timesheets and invoices may seem to you like a small part of the "product" of a representation, because many clients will be unable to evaluate the skill level of your substantive work product, they may view your invoice as representative of the quality of your legal work.

In the interest of providing excellent client service, consider not just what you bill but also what you *do not* bill. Many lawyers, for example, do not bill for every short conversation with a client. If that is your habit, make sure your invoice reflects each of the unbilled conversations in the same detail that you would use if you were going to charge for them, but marked "No Charge." Likewise, if you choose to write off time that was appropriately incurred but that you conclude should not be billed (correcting an error you made, perhaps), that time should be reflected on the invoice as well, with the "No Charge" designation. The same approach applies when you reduce the time charged to the client. Communicate clearly.

Consider too what expenses are appropriate to charge to the client. Your engagement letter should spell out which expenses may be billed, but consider writing off certain charges in an expensive representation. Clients may not be delighted to receive an invoice for $25,000 in legal fees plus a $15.95 cost addition for overnight mail. Each matter and each practice will approach the topic of expenses differently, but you should consider using a rule of reason in deciding what to charge to clients. A cost–shifting decision that saves the client even a small amount of money can be the sort of gesture that generates significant good will. When you choose not to bill a certain expense to the client you should be certain, of course, to reflect that on the invoice.

Facilitate Your Work with Your Clients

Anything you can do to make it easier for your clients to do business with you is likely to be well received by them. For example, you might consider having a client extranet or some secured online space in which client documents can be stored and reviewed. You might use an online workspace that allows you, your staff, and your clients to collaborate on documents without having to e-mail them back and forth or to contend with hard–copy edits. You might introduce your clients to every member of your staff or provide staff biographical sketches online so your clients know to whom they are speaking when they call. Whatever methods you choose, provide them to your clients as a way to facilitate communication and work together, and ask your clients what else they would like you to implement.

One simple way to help your clients is to prepare an orientation document to provide at the beginning of each new matter. Designed to be a physical reminder of the conversation you will have with the client, this document will serve as "Frequently Asked Questions" for how the matter may proceed, how to client should expect to communicate with you and your office, and what the client may expect from you. Simply providing such a document (assuming it is well-designed) may speak volumes to your clients about the care you put into each representation.

Understand Your Client's Business

Regardless of your area of practice, even when your client's business is not at the center of a matter (if, for instance, you are representing a parent in a custody dispute), in most cases the client's business, career, or work will be somehow relevant to the matter. It is important to the client that you understand enough about his business to appreciate the impact of your representation on that business. In fact, most clients desire lawyers who are sufficiently engaged in and aware of their business matters in order to proactively address developments that may affect the business and to make recommendations.

If you intend to build a book of business composed of clients in a particular industry, you would be well advised to spend some time learning about that industry and keeping up with its recent developments. Subscribe to relevant magazines, set a Google Alert for industry news, and consider joining an industry association. If you expect your clients to come from a wide variety of businesses, you will want to employ your listening skills in initial meetings so that you can learn about each new trade. Ask questions. While it is helpful for you to have an understanding of a potential client's business, simply showing interest and asking insightful questions will demonstrate that you seek to know enough about your clients to give well–rounded advice, not advice that is limited solely to the narrow issue at hand with the attitude that the context is someone else's problem.

Spend Time with Your Clients

To deepen your client relationships, you might consider spending time with clients in a social setting or (where appropriate) by visiting their place of business to develop a more full understanding of their business. Both kinds of visits give you an opportunity to talk with your clients to learn more about them on a personal level and on a level that may help you to appreciate more fully the concerns and desires that impact the project(s) on which you are working.

When you schedule a meeting with a client that is devoted to developing the relationship, and particularly when you let the client know that you are not billing for the meeting, you convey the impression that you value the client's business and that you want to serve the client as well as possible. You also set yourself in position to find out through casual conversation how you might better serve that client and about additional needs you might meet.

To identify how best to spend your social and non–

billable time in building client relationships, select your top three to five clients. These are the clients with whom you most like working, whose billings make up a substantial amount of your income, and/or who refer the most work to you. Find out whether these clients enjoy social time with their lawyers and if so, what they enjoy doing. Some might prefer attending sporting events, others might enjoy going to the symphony, and yet others might like best talking with you only on an "as needed" basis about the projects you are handling for them. You will never know without asking. Similarly, some of the clients for whom you are handling a business matter might like you to tour their office, meet various personnel, and do some "on the job" learning about their processes, their customers, and their competitors. Spending this time with your clients can give you insight that will help to inform your representation, and it will also help you to get to know your client (or your corporate client's representatives) on a more personal basis through business–related conversation.

Having determined who your top clients are and how to strengthen your relationships with them, you can adapt this approach for the rest of your clientele. If, for example, your practice centers on estate planning and you write a will for a client of modest means with little expectation of future business from that client, it would not be a good investment of your time to wine and dine him. However, you might consider setting aside a few minutes at the beginning or end of a meeting just to chat with such a client to build a personal (albeit limited) connection with him and to demonstrate that you appreciate the opportunity to serve him. Doing so takes little effort and could pay off when that client mentions you to friends and neighbors with similar needs.

Demonstrate Your Leadership

In the historical model of attorney–client relationships, the lawyer was the expert. Clients would select a lawyer, turn the matter over to that person and her team, and the lawyer would be responsible for resolving the matter and delivering the result to the client. Of course, clients were consulted along the way, but the lawyer took the role as expert to mean that she was in charge of the representation and, though the client might make certain decisions that would influence the direction of the representation, most of the strategy and execution was left to the lawyer. This model still applies in some representations, but today many attorney/client relationships are shifting to a new model.

In this new model, attorney and client partner to identify the ultimate goal for the matter and to find ways to reach it. The lawyer remains the expert with substantive legal knowledge and experience, but rather than being captain of the ship (with the client cast as a mere passenger to be ferried safely to port), the lawyer works *with* her client throughout the representation.

Lawyers must be confident leaders.

The client may dictate certain parameters (including the goal, any circumscriptions on the approach, the budget, the staffing, and frequency and mode of communications), and the client will make most of the decisions with the lawyer's guidance. "Here's what we're going to do" will be replaced by, "Here's what I recommend." And in a weak economy and market, law firm lawyers may discover that their work becomes more limited, with in–house counsel or well–educated non–lawyers performing ministerial and low–level substantive tasks that outside lawyers might previously have handled.

The result of these changes is that lawyers must be confident leaders. A client may believe that his lawyer is a knowledgeable expert based on credentials and reputation, and that client will want to see the lawyer's leadership skills in the course of the representation. Qualities such as strategic and systems thinking, integrity, interpersonal facility, and decisiveness will provide clients with more comfort during a representation.

Deliver Extra Value to Your Clients

Look for ways you can deliver extra value to your clients. By providing some assistance, promotion, or service to your client that is over and above the legal services you have agreed to provide, you demonstrate the importance you place on your client relationships generally and on that client specifically.

Providing extra value might mean sending articles relevant to your clients' area of business or industry, discussing the impact of new legal developments on your client's business affairs or operations, or proactively raising an area of concern that your client may not have spotted. It might also mean making introductions to other professionals in your network or helping your client identify candidates for an open position in the client's business or on a Board with which she is involved. My client Fred, a patent attorney, created a client education system through which he delivered information about the patent process and more general business issues that would interest inventors and introduced resources for other business services.

Offering substantive workshops to your clients may

also provide added value as well as potentially opening opportunities for additional work. When you lead these workshops, be sure to distinguish which issues the client can handle himself with appropriate education and guidance and which issues call for legal advice. This approach assists clients in knowing when they must call for help, increasing the chance that you will learn about upcoming issues early enough to fully address them. Equally importantly, educating clients so that they can handle matters that do not require your input will help to build confidence in you as a leader who tells your clients what they need to know even when doing so may go against your own economic interest.

Ask yourself what opportunities exist to assist your client outside the scope of your engagement, and watch for questions or comments from clients that could signal such opportunities. One helpful approach is to maintain a file of client questions and to review it periodically to look for common concerns. When you spot a question that clients often ask, consider how you might answer that question for future clients even before they ask.

Conduct Client Satisfaction Interviews or Surveys

Unless you ask, your clients are unlikely to volunteer their level of satisfaction, with two exceptions: those who are effusive in praise and those who are dissatisfied to the point of considering terminating the relationship. The vast majority of your clients will be somewhere between those two extremes, and it is important to check in with them to find out where they fall on the satisfaction spectrum. Clients very often will move their legal business to another lawyer without ever raising points of dissatisfaction. Asking how they view the way you are representing them may help you to uncover problems before they threaten the relationship.

These conversations can be quite formal (indeed, you could hire a consultant whose sole purpose is to measure client satisfaction), or they can be more casual. In many instances, the best approach is to ask your clients periodically how satisfied they are with what you are doing to meet their legal needs and with how you are providing those services.

Priority #2: Former Clients and Referral Sources

The second priority for business development efforts is former clients and referral sources. These contacts already know and, presumably, like and trust you. Maintaining contact through the approaches discussed in Part II, *infra,* is the key to further developing relationships and staying top–of–mind with these contacts.

You might also consider interviewing former clients or requesting they complete a survey to determine how satisfied they were with your service and how you might improve. Getting an accurate impression of a former client's satisfaction may not be simple, however, since the representation is by definition completed and there is little motivation for a former client to take the time to respond to your questions.

Priority #3:
"Warm" Potential Clients
and Referral Sources

If you have some connection to a potential client or a contact that might be in a likely position to refer business to you, consider these individuals to be "warm" contacts. They do not yet know, like, or trust you, but if you are introduced by someone in whom they have confidence, you are more likely to be able to develop a relationship with greater speed than without such an introduction. These are the ideal targets for the activities discussed in Part II, *infra,* which are designed to move strategically selected acquaintances into closer association.

Priority #4:
Strangers

Most lawyers who plan to engage in rainmaking activity think first about bringing in new business from potential clients who have no current association with the firm. However, converting complete strangers into clients is by far the most arduous form of business development. It is necessary to determine the potential client's needs and to match your abilities to those needs—assuming that those needs are not currently being met by another lawyer—and, raising the level of difficulty yet further, the process of getting to be known, liked, and trusted begins at ground zero. While strangers do become clients, for many practices the path is significantly longer and less direct than the path from warm contact to client. Wooing strangers should be the lowest priority task in business development activity because it has the lowest potential of yielding new business at any given time. However, continually growing your network and refreshing it with strangers who may advance to warm contacts and then clients or referral sources is a critical aspect of business development.

The Bottom Line for Reluctant Rainmakers

When evaluating your investment in business development activities, always recognize that closer professional relationships are more likely to yield new business. Focus most of your time and energy on current and former clients, move next to referral sources and warm contacts, and focus last on strangers. Because clients typically prefer to work with lawyers whom they know, like, and trust, relationships are paramount to rainmaking success.

Chapter 3

Create Your Business Development Plan

Before diving into rainmaking activity to yield new business and new clients, one final preparatory step is required. Creating a business development plan produces a roadmap for your efforts. As observed in Lewis Carroll's *Alice in Wonderland,* "If you don't know where you're going, any road will get you there." When you take the time to identify specifically what kinds of clients and work you want to generate, you start the process of defining your strategy for bringing in the business you seek and pinpointing which tactics you might employ to carry out that strategy. Two steps (each with sub–steps) are necessary to craft a business development plan: self-assessment and planning. This chapter will consider each in turn.

When I begin a coaching engagement with a would–be rainmaker, my client will often be eager to jump over these preparatory steps and to move directly into action. Doing so is a mistake that actually costs time. Without laying a strategic foundation for rainmaking, you may find that you invest time and energy in activities that fail to deliver the results you expect. Spending just an hour or two planning will almost invariably produce better results. The following pages walk you through each step, and provide questions to consider as well as examples. Please give serious attention to these questions and do not assume that you already know the answers, unless you have mulled over these precise questions recently. To download the Business Development Plan Generator that you can complete during this assessment process, visit http://www.TheReluctantRainmaker.com.

> ***Creating a business development plan produces a roadmap for your efforts.***

Pre-Planning Self-Assessment

Define Your Specialty Area(s)

What are the substantive areas of practice in which you spend most of your time? The answer to this question may seem as simple as writing down your practice group area—intellectual property litigation or estate planning, for example—but you should take the inquiry further. Rather than intellectual property litigation, be clear that your practice encompasses trademark, trade secret, and copyright litigation, that it excludes patent litigation, and that you sometimes address employment issues ancillary to a trade secret matter. Rather than using a description as broad as estate planning, be explicit about whether you do any specific kind of planning such as special needs trusts or estate planning that affects family businesses.

The more narrowly you draw your specialty, the easier you will find it to establish your credentials, visibility, and reputation in your field of practice. A well–defined specialty also makes it simpler to describe what you do when making new connections. The more clearly you are able to express the kind of work you do, the better others will be able to know whether they have now or will likely have in the future a matter that falls within your area of expertise. Potential referral sources are also much more likely to make viable referrals to you if they understand what kind of matter you handle.

If you serve more than one area of practice, some further consideration is necessary here. You may adapt your practice description to your audience—emphasizing your estate planning practice when meeting financial planners and family law when meeting therapists, for example. You might also consider designing an umbrella description that encompasses the breadth of your practice, such as (continuing the example) "a birth–to–death family lawyer." Chapter 12 discusses how to introduce yourself and to talk about your practice, but that discussion will draw on the practice description you build into your business development plan now.

Finally, you might consider whether continuing in more than one or two areas of practice makes sense. In today's market, and for many years, the trend toward specialization has taken center stage among practitioners and clients alike. It is possible to be an accomplished and respected general practitioner, of course, but certain barriers exist for general practitioners that simply do not exist for more focused practitioners Many clients and referral sources will prefer to select those they perceive to be specialists, on the theory that a specialist is more likely to be well–versed in the finer points of a matter and more likely to be aware of the latest developments in the area. Beyond sheer reputation management, practitioners who do not focus in a particular substantive area may face more difficulty in practice because of the need to shift from topic to topic and to reach competency in multiple areas.

Sometimes the best answer is to streamline your practice by ensuring that the substantive areas in which you practice are somehow connected or symbiotic. For instance, family law and estate planning may coexist in harmony, since both practices afford you the opportunity to get to know your clients and to create trust on a personal level. Moreover, clients often need to revise their wills following a divorce, so you may have a natural opportunity to help a client in both areas. Your areas of specialty need not be quite that closely related, but look for synergy between or among your practice fields and consider whether a client would find it logical that you would work in both areas. By setting your specialty areas in this way, you create opportunities for cross–marketing within your own practice.

> ***In today's market, the trend toward specialization has taken center stage among practitioners and clients alike.***

You should consider what areas of practice are "hot" and are generating plenty of opportunities as you make decisions about how to define your practice. Remember, though, that most areas of practice are somewhat cyclical, and that today's hot areas may well be tomorrow's cold ones. One strategy to address this issue is to select fields that react differently to changes in the economic climate, such as real estate and bankruptcy, or to ensure that one of your areas of practice is resistant to recession. No practice area is recession–proof (if only because no industry is recession–proof and individuals' needs may wax and wane based on the economy) but litigation and intellectual property will likely generate at least modest billings during even the most difficult circumstances.

Take some time to write down your practice areas in detail. Whether you decide to focus on a single field or to be a general practitioner, describe specifically the scope of matters you can handle. Consider as well how you might help a referral source to recognize when a matter would be a good fit for your practice.

Finally, after drafting the description of your practice, give some thought to what you most enjoy doing. One benefit of assuming responsibility for generating your own client work is that you get to choose work that is interesting to you. While you will want to choose practice areas that will let you pay your bills despite an economic downturn, you must build a practice that interests and engages you. A lawyer who is not interested in her practice area is more susceptible to burnout and less likely to excel in practice. By the same token, clients want to work with lawyers who show some enthusiasm for their work. Your work need not be your passion in life (though lawyers who do feel that level of engagement often rise to the top of their firms and fields), but you must find enough meaning and enjoyment in your work to put in the energy and hours required. How do you feel when you read the practice definition you drafted?

How Would You Describe Yourself as a Lawyer?

The task here is to take a comprehensive look at your

practice. Consider your practice competencies and skills, and then take it a step further. What client service habits set you apart from other lawyers? What non–billable activities bear on your work or bring some benefit to your clients? (If, for example, you serve on the Board of Directors for a nonprofit and are able to make introductions to other Board members on behalf of your clients, clients may view that service as a substantial benefit to them.) What is your work style, and how does that affect your clients? What sets you apart from other lawyers with a similar practice and similar clients?

All of these attributes bring something (positive or negative) to your work with clients, and the better grip you have on those attributes and their consequences the better you will be able to position yourself *vis à vis* new clients or existing clients who may bring you new business. In traditional marketing language, what you bring to your clients and your practice creates your "unique selling proposition" or "USP," which provides a quick answer to the question why someone should retain you rather than another lawyer.

A word of caution: while many attributes and approaches to client service may set you apart from other practitioners, be careful not to choose a generality as a point of differentiation. You may very well be strategic and client-focused, but the vast majority of lawyers would probably make the same claim. If you cannot be specific in a way that would distinguish you from others, you have not identified your USP.

We will return to this concept in subsequent chapters, allowing you to flesh out a USP that will support the development and implementation of your business development plan.

Who Are Your Ideal Clients?

Now that you have a practice description drafted, we need to look at the clients you are targeting. Again, part of the description may flow from your area of practice. If, for example, your practice is limited to representing plaintiffs in medical malpractice cases, some aspects of your ideal client are predefined. Other attributes, however, may remain open for your choices. Consider these questions:

- Are your ideal clients located in a specific geographic region?
- Do your ideal clients have a particular demographic description? Are they mostly men or women, young or old, professional or blue–collar workers?
- Do your ideal clients have a psychographic description? (Psychographics are attributes that describe lifestyle, attitudes, beliefs, values, and the like.)
- What legal concerns do your ideal clients share?
- What other attributes do your ideal clients have in common?

If you have trouble profiling your ideal client, list your top five to ten clients. When identifying those clients, look not only at the revenue each has generated, but also at how much you have enjoyed working with each. Your "top client" list may include some clients who have generated significant billings but with whom you do not enjoy working: these are not ideal clients. Identifying non–ideal clients is valuable because it will help you recognize other non–ideal would–be clients in the future. The remainder of the clients on your list, those with whom you enjoyed working and who generated significant revenue, are your ideal clients. At the risk of stating the obvious, you want to bring in more ideal clients.

> ***Place a priority on connecting with and developing your referral sources.***

Because few clients are truly ideal, some lawyers become concerned that identifying ideal clients means that their practice will be limited or less profitable. Creating a profile of your ideal client increases the chance of working with those clients, simply because you will know how to recognize them and how to describe them to others who might be in a position to make referrals to you. You may choose to fill your practice with a mix of ideal and non–ideal clients for the sake of income. Nevertheless, by describing your ideal client with as much precision as possible and then using that description as explained in subsequent chapters, you will raise the percentage of ideal clients with whom you work.

Who Are Your Referral Sources?

As described in Chapter 2, you should place a priority on connecting with and developing your referral sources because they already know, like, and trust you. Perhaps you have already received referrals; if so, list the sources and their common attributes, as you did with ideal clients. If not, think about what kind of connection might be most likely to yield a referral for you. For instance, if you specialize in estate planning for high net–worth individuals, you might seek referrals from financial planners who work with those clients but probably not from a banker at a branch in a low–income part of town. The goal here is to develop a profile of those most likely to refer clients and matters to you so that you can direct your efforts toward reaching them. You may even be able to take this inquiry a step further and list people you know who match the profile you have identified.

What Are Your Communications Strengths?

As you will see in Part II, numerous avenues exist to reach your ideal clients and referral sources. The most successful rainmakers typically identify a handful of business development activities and implement them repeatedly, rather than trying to use every possible method. All of those activities require communicating in some form with a target audience, so identifying your communications strengths will help you realize what tactics are most likely to be effective for you. Do you enjoy writing? Do audiences give you rave reviews when you make a formal presentation? Do you prefer meeting and talking with groups, or would you rather have one–on–one conversations? When you know your communications strengths, you can decide which subset of rainmaking tactics is most likely to be effective for you and, therefore, which activities will form your strongest starting point.

You may have heard somewhere along the way that a certain activity—networking, perhaps—is critical for rain-making success and that everyone who hopes to bring in new business must learn to master that activity if they are to have any chance of succeeding. Not true. Some rainmakers will excel at networking, some at writing, some at speaking, others at meeting one–on–one with members of a target group, and so on.

Rather than elevating any single activity to "must do" status, start by claiming your current strengths and working to improve them. Recent research demonstrates that, although one can in theory become masterful in most any task, improving strengths brings quicker and easier results than improving weaknesses. To accomplish your rainmaking goals, then, focus on your strengths and the activities you enjoy most.

Doubt the research? Think about what happens when a lawyer takes on a task that he does not enjoy. Imagine that Rich has decided to network in two industry groups in which his clients and ideal clients participate, even though he considers himself to be an introvert and has avoided networking in the past. Initially, he will attend with enthusiasm, having decided that attending these meetings will help him to grow his practice. Chances are that Rich will eventually dread going to the meetings, and because he would rather not attend, he will find justifications to skip them—here and there, at first, but every missed meeting will make it easier for him not to return. The justifications will likely appear to be entirely legitimate: the press of billable work, the need to keep up with recent developments in some hot area of practice, even spending more time with his family.

Putting less time into meeting with these groups ensures that the results will be sub-par, and Rich will not improve his networking skills or experience success that would encourage him to keep working at it. With poor results from an unpleasant task, who would willingly continue? Presto, Rich concludes that he may as well stop trying to network. If he has bought into the idea that networking, which he has now concluded he cannot do well, is the secret to rainmaking success, Rich's "failure" may undermine his confidence in his ability to bring in new business.

Rich created his own failure by choosing an activity that does not come naturally and then by rationalizing his disengagement from that activity, which guaranteed that he would not get the good results he was seeking. But he is unlikely to see that he set himself up to fail. Instead, he will focus on the failure and conclude that perhaps he cannot bring in new business after all.

Contrast that scenario to one in which Nancy, who loves meeting new people, talking in group settings, and following up one–on–one to deepen relationships, decides to join industry groups that her clients attend. Unlike Rich, Nancy will likely look forward to the meetings, and when work or another commitment crops up and threatens to prevent her from making it to a meeting, Nancy will probably do everything possible to keep the appointment. She will likely enjoy some of the connections she makes, which will prompt her to follow up with those people outside the group meetings. Over time, she will develop relationships that will enrich her professionally and personally and may lead (directly or through referral) to new business, especially if she also spends time learning about the tactics of successful networkers and lays her strategy well.

Improving strengths brings quicker and easier results than improving weaknesses.

Because she has drawn on an area of natural strength, Nancy is predisposed to succeed with networking. Her success will reinforce itself, she will continue to attend the meetings and meet other members, and she will conclude that networking is a perfect tactic for her—particularly when she does receive a new matter as a result.

The only difference between Rich and Nancy is that Nancy identified and used a natural strength, while Rich took on networking even though he knew he disliked it and considered it a weakness. Could Rich have succeeded despite these challenges? Of course. He would have had to overcome his dislike, however, or to combat it before every single meeting and to be vigilant in not allowing himself to escape his networking duty despite excellent justifications for doing so. That is a steep mountain to climb, and Rich would be far better advised to select another activity as the backbone of his business development plan.

Obstacles and Opportunities

The economic crisis of 2008 and 2009 revealed unique challenges in the legal industry as a whole, and those challenges have lingered and in many ways deepened in the years since. Changes affecting practice occur constantly. Shifts in the hot areas of practice, in technological solutions to facilitate practice and client communication and collaboration, and new cost-cutting staffing methods (such as offshoring) are just a few examples of the changes that have faced lawyers in the last few years. Competitive changes have multiplied as well, as firm mergers and closings have, in some cases, impacted entire legal communities. What changes have created obstacles or opportunities in your practice and for your clients?

Obstacles and opportunities are often closely related. For example, you may see an obstacle to the growth of your practice arise if your clients are requesting alternative billing arrangements and you bill strictly by hours. An inherent opportunity exists in that situation, however: you might discover that changing the way you bill actually increases your revenue, or that pursuing a different kind of client less interested in alternative arrangements brings you more ideal clients. As you find obstacles in practice or in business development, look for the opportunities that accompany them. Some coaching clients make a practice of noting obstacles in writing so that they prime themselves to come up with creative solutions.

What Commitments Must You Meet?

Before moving to your goals, make a note of the commitments that you have already accepted. Consider professional commitments (beginning, most likely, with billable hours) as well as personal. The reason for listing these obligations is two–fold. First, you may discover that some commitments should be broken. For instance, if you have agreed to chair a fundraiser that is unrelated to your practice and that does not represent an important aspect of your personal life, perhaps you should find a substitute chair and back out gracefully.

Second, when you have identified your non–negotiable commitments, you know how much of your time and energy is already dedicated elsewhere, which helps you to be realistic about what else you can take on in the interest of business development. How much time is left over in your schedule? If you find that your available time is insufficient for instituting new business development activity, you will need to adjust either the way you spend your time or your rainmaking activities and goals. Part IV focuses on time management for rainmakers.

What Has Worked in the Past?

If you have successfully engaged in business development activities in the past, what has worked well? Did a client retain you for additional business or refer a new client to you? Who else referred business to you? Through which activities did you meet new clients or referral sources? List all of the activities that, directly or by referral, resulted in new engagements for you.

If you work in a law firm, note the more senior lawyers for whom you did work and any colleagues who introduced you to their clients. Also note, even if no business resulted, the activities that added to your credentials, including articles you wrote, CLE or other presentations you made, and law or legally–related classes you taught. List also the notable matters that you worked on in the last year. How might you summarize those engagements in your biographical sketch to make them useful for business development?

In this part of your self–assessment, your goal is to collect in one place a list of all of your business development activities over the past year so that you can evaluate the effectiveness of those activities. With the benefit of hindsight, would you exclude anything you did? What would you increase or add to the mix? Make notes, because you will draw on what you have learned in the past to guide your approach in the future.

Congratulations! You have now completed the self–assessment part of crafting your business development plan. It is time to begin the actual planning.

Planning for Rainmaking Success

What Are Your Goals?

First, set your rainmaking goals. Be as specific as possible. What type and size of matters would you like to land? Would you prefer to handle all of the work on the matter, to be responsible for it and to allow others to assist in performing the work, or to pass on all responsibility for the substantive work, retaining only a client relations role? What is the dollar value of the book of business you would like to grow? In brief, what do you want to accomplish as a rainmaker in the next year to 18 months?

Describe your ultimate goals here, not the steps required to reach those goals. For example, as a sole practitioner, you might decide that you want to reshape your estate planning practice to focus on high net-worth individuals, yielding revenue of $450,000, while reducing the number of hours you bill each week. If you're working in a larger firm, you might set a goal to increase your book of business to $800,000, with a clientele comprised of small–cap companies needing help with technology licensing and patent protection, and with you as the primary billing lawyer using support from a junior associate.

Note that if you are a new lawyer relying on more senior lawyers to assign you to cases, your goals may be directed primarily toward credential– and reputation–enhancing activities such as professional development, article writing, networking with colleagues at your firm, and networking with bar association or client industry groups. Especially if you are working in a large firm, your seniority in practice will likely have a strong influence on the goals you set. Review Chapter 17 for more information.

What Is Your Strategy?

Having set your goals, consider your strategy for reaching them. Strategy represents your overall plan for achieving your goals, your big picture approach, and a clear direction for forward movement. Strategy can be complex multi–layered plans for accomplishing objectives and may give consideration to tactics, but strategy is the 30,000–foot view of your path, whereas tactics comprise the actual roadmap. What strategy would be effective for reaching the goals you have set?

> ***Strategy represents your overall plan for achieving your goals, your big picture approach, and a clear direction for forward movement.***

Continuing the previous example, your strategy might include establishing yourself as the go–to patent lawyer in your community in a particular field of technology and marketing your services based on that reputation to companies that have graduated from an incubator into full operation. You could accomplish that strategy in a multitude of ways, and setting the strategy simply identifies your guiding principles for future rainmaking effort.

You may want to identify more than one strategy, because sometimes the plans you expect to be a sure success will fizzle out for reasons outside your control. When you identify more than one path to achieve your goals, you allow for setbacks and diversify the opportunities to succeed. An example of a multi–part relationship-building strategy might be contacting former clients to offer an article or checklist that contains useful information about an area of the law that relates to them or their business, meeting with current clients to do an audit in an area outside the scope of your current engagement, and setting up meetings with people you have identified who might be good referral sources.

> ***Setting a strategy gives you a roadmap to follow, and lets you plug each of the action items you choose to implement into a cohesive, coordinated rainmaking approach.***

When you set a strategy, you are defining your approach and setting the stage to select the tasks that will implement that approach. Different from goal–setting, strategy lays out the overarching map that you will use to reach your objectives. In a sense, you create a test against which to measure potential action steps. If you set a strategy to contact former clients to offer an article or checklist that they will find useful, you will undertake related tasks such as writing useful articles and placing telephone calls to former clients to renew your relationship and make your offer. You will consider whether you should call former clients by telephone, invite them to a social event, send a mass mailing, or otherwise reach out to make your offer. Your thoughts and action plan will center around how you can generate useful content and how you will then get that content into your former clients' hands. Other rainmaking approaches will be less important to you, not because they are necessarily ineffective, but because they are not in line with your strategy.

Strategy sets the *why* for all of your rainmaking actions. Why should you speak at an industry association meeting? Because you have set a strategy of using speaking to raise your profile in your area of practice. Why should you identify small medical device companies and research their patent portfolios? Because you have set a strategy of approaching patent–rich companies and offering to serve as their part–time inside patent counsel. Why should you attend a meeting of the National Association of Personal Financial Advisors? Unless doing so will advance a strategy you have set, you should not.

Strategic planning is like the process of deciding whether to use a passing or running game plan, to use a football analogy: if your plan calls for your team to rely primarily on a running game, you will call in your fastest runners without questioning their throwing skills. When you move to tactical planning, you will decide which players to bring into the game and you will decide which plays to run. When you focus on the strategy, however, you will limit your inquiry to determining which overall approach is most likely to capitalize on your team's strengths and to take advantage of your opponents' weaknesses.

Before contacting me, some of my clients have skipped the strategy–laying step, and the result is that they move forward with a variety of uncoordinated activities. They may write articles, but lacking a strategy that incorporates writing, the articles are published but not used, for example, as the basis for a client seminar. They engage in networking, but without a strategic plan, they may not know which individuals (by name or profile) to seek out or what they should do after meeting those people. Setting a strategy gives you a roadmap to follow and lets you plug each of the action items you choose to implement into a cohesive, coordinated rainmaking approach.

Determine Your Tactical Approach

Tactics, the action steps through which strategies are executed, refer to activities created and selected to reach specific and measurable objectives. Setting your tactics forms the bridge between strategic planning and execution. For example, imagine that you set a goal of developing a $750,000 book of business representing high net worth individuals in divorce actions. Your strategy might call for you to reach out to financial advisors of high net worth individuals. To implement that strategy, you might use tactics such as joining and attending meetings of a financial planning association, following up one–on–one with the members you meet and then delivering relevant substantive information to them, such as articles or checklists that you have written and that you expect, based on your conversation, your contacts to find useful.

Part II of *The Reluctant Rainmaker,* the Rainmaker's Toolkit, discusses a wide variety of tactics. Select two to three tactical approaches per strategy. As you select the actions you plan to take, make sure that you have or can create enough implementation time, and consider how to use the ideas on systems and routines presented in Part IV to develop some processes that will operate without requiring your continuous personal input. By doing so, you will increase your effective time while minimizing the time required to achieve results. Note too, as you set each action step, which tasks you could delegate to an assistant to maximize your time.

Implement Your Plan

Having created your business development plan, your next steps should be clear. Set yourself up for success from the beginning by doing the necessary preparatory work (such as identifying meeting times and dates for the groups you plan to join) or assigning someone else to do it. Calendar relevant dates and reminders, with enough advance warning so that you do not find yourself slamming into a meeting or opportunity only to discover that you neglected to do the preliminary work that would have increased your chances for success.

One mistake that lawyers often make when implementing a business development plan is in deciding to go it alone. Create accountability for yourself, and arm yourself with a mentor, coach, or group to help you figure out how to overcome the obstacles that will inevitably occur. By doing so, you significantly reduce the risk that you will let your rainmaking plans slide, even when you get busy or overwhelmed. Chapter 1 includes advice on how to identify and select your accountability and support partners.

Create a tracking system so you will have a convenient record to determine what has been most and least effective in your plan.

Finally, create a tracking system for yourself so that at the end of the year you will have a convenient record to review as you determine what has been most and least effective in your plan. Your system can be as simple as creating a table that tracks date, activity, result, and follow–up (visit http://www.TheReluctantRainmaker.com for a sample table), or it can be much more complex, using specialized sales software. Choose a system that is simple for you to access and use so that you remove excuses to delay tracking your results. Do not neglect this step or delay your tracking to the point that you are forced to rely on memory alone, and recollection is rarely sufficient for evidence-based decision making.

As is the case with timesheets, contemporaneous recordings are the easiest and most reliable. Tracking through the year is also helpful to create an additional source of accountability, so that (for example) you have a chance to notice that you have issued only four lunch invitations over a quarter, which will allow you to step up your efforts in the next quarter so that you stay on track.

The Bottom Line for Reluctant Rainmakers

Clichés are repeated because they bear at least a kernel of truth, and the old saw that failing to plan is planning to fail is time–tested and spot-on. If you are a reluctant rainmaker who has decided that now is the time to get started, you may be tempted to skip the planning step and to jump into action. Doing so almost guarantees that your activity will be poorly focused and that your results will be scattershot. Just as a skyscraper must be built on a strong physical foundation to stand, your business development activities must be grounded in a plan that takes account of your strengths, goals, and commitments. To break the reluctant rainmaker mold and to experience success in your business development efforts, take the required time to plan and set yourself up for triumph.

Chapter 4

Prepare Your Written Marketing Materials

Your potential clients and referral sources come to know you in one of three ways: by meeting you, by your reputation (or word of mouth), and by your marketing materials. Regardless of how an initial connection occurs, you will certainly find it helpful to have strong written materials prepared. Although the potential scope of those materials is broad, this chapter's discussion is limited to the three essentials: your business card, your biographical sketch, and your website. Before preparing these materials, confirm that they meet any criteria that may be set forth in your state's ethics rules. Be sure as well to review Chapters 6, 7, and 13 for a discussion of other written material such as articles, blogs, and newsletters.

Business Cards

Even in today's electronics–driven world, a business card is a key tool for your business development efforts. Your business card may serve as an introduction, if passed on by a contact to a third party, and it may also serve as a contact's tangible reminder of a meeting with you. Be sure that you have cards with you at all times, even if you do not anticipate an opportunity to use them. Having business cards ready to offer creates a low–key impression that you are always prepared; failing to have them when needed may suggest the opposite. Make it your habit to tuck a few cards into your wallet, your briefcase, and perhaps even your cell phone case if possible, and carry a business card case as well. Consider the message you send with the card carrier you choose, too: what message do you send if you fill your business card case as full as possible? One interpretation is that you have so many cards available because others rarely ask for them. A small point, to be sure, but you can avoid creating that impression simply by putting in a few cards and having a convenient reserve if necessary.

> ***A business card is a key tool for your business development efforts.***

If you are practicing in a large firm, the firm most likely has prescribed the form and content of your business card. Whatever your practice setting, if you have the latitude to design your own card, consider what your contacts and referral sources might expect to see. If your clients are large corporations, for example, they will expect a conservative card with black imprinting (thermography or engraving) on cream or white card stock. If you represent technology start–up companies, however, you probably have more leeway and could design a card that is tailored specifically to your market. Judicious use of color and design can help you create a card that will speak to your target clients. Let your clientele be your guide as to any atypical elements you may incorporate.

If you would like to differentiate your card from those of other lawyers, consider using a card with rounded edges or orienting the text in portrait layout (across the narrow axis of the card) rather than in landscape. Depending on your practice area and the level of conservatism your clients are likely to expect, you might experiment with a square card or one that is larger than normal. If you do use an unusual shape or size, be aware that your contacts may be unable to treat your card like the other cards they receive—putting it into their own business card case for safekeeping, for instance—and remember that you will be unable to use standard document folders that include cut-outs for standard business cards.

Consider carefully the impact that choosing a unique business card may have. If you are just beginning your practice and have an opportunity to design your card, unless you are certain about using unconventional colors or design elements, you cannot go wrong by starting with a conventional, conservative business card. In time, you may choose to show more of your personality, or the personality that matches your ideal clients, but you will find it easier to move from conventional to unconventional than vice versa.

The card itself should be heavy stock (100 pounds is a good weight) and matte. Glossy cards may look nice, but you will find it almost impossible to write on them (a resource or telephone number for a referral you make) unless you happen to carry a permanent marker with you. Many people make a habit of writing a note on a business card they receive, and you may find that having a glossy card makes notations more difficult for those who receive it.

Once you have selected the physical layout of your card, consider the text. Some items are obvious: your name, your firm or business name, address, telephone, website, and e-mail address. If you use a tag line for your practice, include that as well. One part of a business card's function is to assist in reinforcing your "brand" or business identity. For that reason, you should include a logo if you use one, and you might consider (depending on your anticipated audience) incorporating your photograph, the URL for your LinkedIn profile page, or your Twitter name.

You may be able to make good use of the back of your card as well. Perhaps you could identify your areas of specialty, or you could list three or four bulleted questions that would help a potential client or a referral source better understand what kinds of engagements you accept. If you offer an e-mailed client newsletter or legal updates (see Chapter 13), you might include a web address for the subscription page. Whatever you choose to include on the back of your card, if anything, ensure that you leave sufficient white space for a contact to jot down a few words about you or for you to note a useful resource and offer that to your contact.

Biographical Sketch

Business cards are typically offered only to those whom you have met in person, though they may be passed on to a third party. Biographical sketches, in contrast, are (must be!) freely available on your firm's website, and recent studies show that biographical pages are the most visited on any attorney website. In the past, clients might have checked legal directories such as Martindale–Hubbell, and a few will do so now. Most likely, potential clients today will rely primarily on what they find in your biographical sketch. As a result, you must have a well–written, credential–packed sketch on your website. Before continuing to read this section, you might want to print a copy of your sketch and grab a red pen.

When is a photograph too old?

Have you ever happened on a biographical sketch and discovered someone who is still using a photograph that was clearly taken some 20 years ago? The camera–averse may prefer to avoid updating an attractive photograph, but imagine what happens when a potential client sees a photograph of a chubby–cheeked 25–year old alongside a biography that details a distinguished 25 years in practice. Enough to derail an engagement? No, probably not, but the dissonance may raise eyebrows. Worse yet, it could create a misimpression of your "brand" or a perception that you neglect details or fail to keep up with changing circumstances. If you wonder whether your photograph is out–of–date, show it to a few colleagues and ask for their honest feedback—and act on it.

First, be sure that your photograph is a reasonably flattering, reasonably accurate representation. Although your credentials and skill undoubtedly matter more than your looks in any hiring decision, the reader's eye will naturally be drawn to your photograph as soon as he looks at your biographical sketch. If you include a photograph in which you look somewhat serious but approachable, the reader will move on to review the text of your sketch. An unflattering photograph may, however, subconsciously influence the reader. Much research supports the proposition that attractive people are more likely to be hired (and to enjoy other benefits in life), though none explicitly extends those findings to a client's decision to hire a lawyer. If your headshot is out of date, or if it does not portray you to your advantage, get a new headshot taken by a professional photographer.

Next, consider what text to include in your biographical sketch. As with business cards, unless you are a sole practitioner, you may find that your formatting options are limited. Whether you follow the format recommended here or your firm's mandated format, be sure that readers can scan your sketch and locate the most important elements: credentials and experience. Your sketch should have a narrative section as well as breakouts or bullet–point lists that highlight certain aspects of your experience.

The most important section of your biographical sketch may be the identification of your practice areas. Drawing on the self-assessment discussed in Chapter 3, list your practice areas or your umbrella statement for your practice. Because the purpose of a biographical sketch is to provide a concise but complete description of your practice, you may choose to include areas of practice in which you have experience that are outside your core practice or core expertise. Although your business development efforts should be directed to bringing in new business in the area(s) of practice in which you specialize or intend to specialize, identifying other areas in which you have handled past matters will be helpful to some clients. Be sure, however, that you are selective and list only those areas in which you have some continuing interest. If, for example, you are an IP litigator and you handled small collections and a few personal injury defense matters at the beginning of your practice, adding those may detract from your current experience and expertise. If you have experience in IP licensing, technology transfer, or complex business litigation, potential clients would likely view those areas as being complementary to your primary practice and even potentially useful in the course of an IP litigation matter. In other words, do not limit your practice areas unduly, but make sure that the areas you do list are relevant to your current practice and not so extensive as to be confusing.

> ***Most readers will want to know what you have accomplished on behalf of your clients, so focus on results.***

The order of the remaining elements of a biographical sketch depends largely on your seniority level. More junior lawyers will likely focus on their education and bar admissions in the first few years of practice, while acquiring the practice experience needed to include representative matters and clients, articles written, and speeches presented. More senior lawyers will focus primarily on their practice experience, relegating education and bar admissions to the end of the sketch because those items become less important after some years in practice. Even if you are a brand new practitioner, however, be sure to include some narrative in your biographical sketch and to update it as often as necessary to begin to flesh out a strong history of your experience. (See Chapter 17 for recommendations specific to junior lawyers working in law firms.)

Assuming that you are not just starting your practice,

the bulk of your narrative should concentrate on your substantive legal experience. This is your opportunity to draw the reader's attention to the core areas of your practice, both by identifying your focal area(s) and by giving a few examples. If you have listed your practice areas elsewhere in your sketch, be sure to do more than just reiterate the list. Add details and key experience highlights that will allow readers to appreciate the scope of your practice. Because most readers will want to know what you have accomplished on behalf of your clients, focus on results. For example, a real estate financing lawyer might include a narrative statement such as, "Assisted top real estate developer in receiving $12.7 million financing for construction of in-town residential/ commercial condominium complex."

You may want to request permission from certain of your clients to identify them in the narrative or in a list of representative clients. (Use good judgment here: requesting permission to include a large corporation by name following a securities offering is appropriate, but asking an individual client for permission to list her name after you defended her in a criminal case is not.) Without permission, use generic descriptions for your clients: top real estate developer, corporation with $2 million in annual revenue, or high net worth individuals, for example.

Your narrative should also include credibility enhancers, such as selected articles you have written, presentations you have delivered, leadership roles in industry, bar, or community organizations, and special skills such as fluency in another language. When including articles or speeches, include those that are most directly related to your focal area of practice, that were published or delivered in a well–recognized forum, and that were relatively recent. You might choose to highlight an older article, however, if it was cited in court decisions or is otherwise particularly notable. Leadership positions in community or industry groups or in bar associations will also enhance your credibility, and a brief description of your involvement should be included in your narrative.

Finally, your narrative may include a mention of previous employment, if appropriate, and potentially some personal information. If you completed military service or other public service, include that in your narrative. If you moved to your current position from another law firm, including that information is probably unnecessary absent unique circumstances. When including personal information (which is by no means required and may be distracting in some instances), select a few interests that are non–controversial or offer some information about your background.

In addition to the matters you highlight in the narrative part of your sketch, create a "Representative Matters" or "Representative Clients" section that lists your significant past representations. You need not list every matter you have handled in the past, but you should list all matters that moved beyond an initial exploratory phase or that achieved significant results for a client. You may identify clients by name with permission or resort to generic descriptions. Other information following your narrative should include bar admissions; articles you have written (including legal alerts and articles published in your firm's newsletter); speeches you have presented; and bar, industry, and community organization memberships. A long list of significant representations, articles, speeches, memberships, and leadership roles will raise your credibility.

Review and update your sketch quarterly. When you have ten to fifteen matters listed, however, become more selective about the projects you include. The narrative section should include your most significant and most impressive matters, and after you achieve critical mass in your bullet–point list, cull or aggregate less substantial matters. For example, if you have settled 25 personal injury cases in the $20,000 to $40,000 range, you might aggregate them into a single bullet–point that reads, "Lead counsel for numerous personal injury cases, obtaining settlements between $20,000 and $40,000 in each," and you would include a $2.4 million settlement in your narrative and as a separate bullet point. You should, of course, continue to add significant matters (as well as all articles, speeches, and leadership positions) to your sketch.

After you have completed your biographical sketch, create a short sketch for use with articles or blog posts you write, for the program for presentations you may deliver, and for your online marketing use. A 100–word biography is the standard, and creating it now will save you substantial time in the future.

Checklist for biographical sketch

- Photograph
- Area(s) of practice
- Narrative, including description of practice area, highlighted representations, education, selected articles/presentations, leadership roles in industry, community, or bar organizations, special skills such as fluency in another language, professional awards received, previous employment, and (optional) personal interests
- Bullet–point list of:
    - Representative matters/clients (breakout)
    - Bar admissions (breakout)
    - Articles written (breakout)
    - Speeches made (breakout)
    - Bar, industry, and community organization memberships

Website

A website is now an absolute necessity for every law firm and sole practitioner. If you are a sole practitioner, the design of your website will be entirely up to you. If you work in a law firm, you may or may not have a voice in the website design or content. Educating yourself on a few basics of Internet marketing will be useful whether you are working with a static website that has remained unchanged since it was launched, an existing website that can be revised and updated, or a website waiting to be built. Numerous books and vendors offer support for lawyers who are establishing their websites, and you should look to those resources for complete information.

> ***A website is now an absolute necessity for every law firm and sole practitioner.***

You should also review the ethics rules of the state(s) in which you practice to ensure that your online presence complies with those limitations. This section is designed only to be a primer, to raise questions that you should consider, and to give you some guidance as you investigate other resources. For more resources, visit http://www.TheReluctantRainmaker.com.

You can spend a great deal of time and money building an attractive site, but your emphasis should be on building a site that is effective for providing information and demonstrating to potential clients that you have substantial expertise. The bare essentials for a good website include an appropriate domain name, a home page with a description of the firm's geographic and service areas, biographical sketches for every lawyer and perhaps for staff members, and contact information including your e-mail and office addresses and telephone number. Optional features include articles, links to useful websites, and options for subscription to an electronic or hard copy newsletter.

Domain Name

The selection of your domain name is probably a simple matter. Choose your firm name, your name, or some accurate descriptor of your area of practice, perhaps in combination with a geographical designation. Make sure that the domain name is easy to say and to type, preferably excluding difficult words or homonyms. Because most people are accustomed to typing ".com" URL and e-mail addresses, you should choose an available .com domain, even if you would prefer to have a domain name that is available only as a .net, .info, or other type of domain. Examples of good domain names include: SmithAndJonesLLC.com, RichardDeutschLawOffice.com, JOMLawAssoc.com and IllinoisPersonalInjuryLawFirm.com. When purchasing your domain name, be sure to purchase domains that cover common misspellings and typographical errors as well.

Home Page

Your website's homepage should offer a short description of the firm's practice. Use a professional but reasonably conversational tone, and avoid legal jargon. Write your text to meet your readers' interest, providing the information and directions that they need rather than focusing all attention on you or the law firm. Compare the number of times that words such as "you" and "your" appear as compared with "I," "we," and "our." The ratio should be heavily weighted toward "you" and "your," or potential clients reviewing your website may conclude that the website offers nothing for them.

A short home page is generally preferable so that readers can quickly scan it, and you should be sure to include "keywords" that will identify your practice area. Keywords are the words that potential clients might enter into Google or other search engines to find your firm, such as "tax attorney Michigan" or "ERISA lawyer San Diego." (See further discussion of keywords, *infra*.) The text on your home page should also direct readers' next steps, perhaps to review the attorneys' biographical sketches or to call the office for an initial consultation.

Biographical Sketches

The previous section addressed how to draft your own biographical sketch, which should appear on your website. For online searching purposes, ensure that your sketch includes the relevant keywords for your practice. If you practice with other lawyers, the firm website should include a search function or easy navigation so that readers trying to locate a specific profile can do so quickly and easily.

Depending on your firm size and practice area, you might consider "introducing" support staff members on your website. While corporate clients might find such inclusion unnecessary and perhaps even distracting, individual clients who consult you on a personal matter may be more comfortable if they know something about the other staff members with whom they may be interacting. For example, if your practice focuses on education law and specifically on creating educational plans for special needs children, your clients might appreciate the opportunity to know something about your staff members before meeting them. Even if you choose not to make your staff members' profiles public by linking them from other pages, consider having brief profiles available on your website so that you can send the URL and a copy of the profile to new clients who will be contacted by or working with those staff members.

Contact Information

You should include a page titled "Contact Us" or "Contact Information" that contains your office's physical address, mailing address, and telephone and fax numbers. Adding a link to Mapquest or Google Maps is especially helpful for those unfamiliar with your office location.

To limit the amount of e-mail spam that you receive, consider placing your e-mail address on your biographical sketch and on the contact page as an image rather than as a link. (Any reasonably savvy web professional will be able to do so, and you can learn to do this easily if you choose to assume the creation and/or maintenance of your website, though doing so is almost certainly not the best use of your time.) Alternatively, you might use a form that allows readers who want to contact you to provide their name and contact information and a message, all of which will be e-mailed to you for response. You should be sure to include disclaimers (that merely contacting an attorney does not create an attorney/client relationship) as appropriate under the ethics rules of the jurisdictions in which you practice.

Optional: Articles and Other Content

Posting articles written by you or other firm lawyers on the firm's website can be useful to establish the firm's and its lawyers' credibility, to provide useful information for potential clients and others who access the content, and (if keywords are used effectively) to raise the website's status with search engines for your area(s) of practice. Content generation is discussed in Part II of this book (see Chapters 6, 7, and 13), and you should consider whether and how you might repurpose any non–work product documents for use on your website.

Useful content for inclusion on a law firm website runs the gamut from articles to videos of presentations. Press releases are a useful marketing strategy for establishing reputation and credibility for the firm and for getting the firm into the news. If your firm issues press releases, they should be published on your website contemporaneously with their issuance. Blogs are another type of content generation for websites, and are discussed at some length in Chapter 7.

> ***Approach the question of what you include on your website with creativity.***

Approach the question of what you might include on your website with creativity, always being mindful of what potential clients would expect to see on their lawyer's website. When you include legal content on your website with articles, video, and press releases, you create a library of materials that potential clients and others who visit your website may find useful and indicative of your expertise.

Optional: Links

Some lawyers and law firms may find it beneficial to offer links to other websites. As with creating a content library, including links becomes a value–added service for potential clients. If you do place links on your website, ensure that they work correctly (because a broken link looks sloppy—not the impression you want to create) and that they are relevant to needs that your clients and potential clients may have. Refrain from including links simply to fill space.

Optional: Newsletter Subscription Forms

Chapter 13 discusses how to create and circulate a newsletter for your contacts' benefit. A newsletter (circulated electronically or in hard copy) can be effective for staying in touch with former clients, referral sources, and potential clients. If you offer a newsletter, be sure that visitors can subscribe themselves directly from every page of your website. Software used for electronic newsletter generation will generate a form that can be placed onto your website, and a website developer can easily create such a form to capture interested visitors' names and addresses for hard copy circulation. Be sure to review the discussion of how to promote your newsletter in Chapter 13 so that you craft your offer correctly on your website. In years past, simple language like "sign up for our newsletter" would almost guarantee a flood of new subscribers. Thanks to the increase in spam, junk mail, and concerns about potential identity theft, website visitors are loathe to provide any personal information (including addresses, physical or electronic) without some inducement.

A Word About Keywords

As previously discussed, keywords are the search terms that computer users enter into Google and other online directories to locate websites of interest. An entire industry exists for search engine optimization ("SEO") and for search engine traffic generated from paid keyword–driven advertisements. If you want to maximize your online marketing, you may find it worthwhile to investigate and hire a consultant in these areas. Doing so can be cost–effective and time–effective, though the initial investment may be somewhat eye–popping. (You must also do full due diligence before hiring an SEO expert, because some use "black hat" tactics that may result in your website being penalized or even removed from Google search results.)

As a simple rule of thumb, unless and until you decide to engage such help, using the relevant keywords in the text of your website will be a good first step. By weaving them into your text in a natural way ("Steve focuses his practice on bankruptcy claims for Denver–area individual clients," for example) you will receive some presence in search engine listings. A blog, which is often naturally rich in its use of appropriate key words, is another way to support SEO. Please visit the http://www.TheReluctanRainmaker.com for further information about keywords and how to use them.

Other Written Marketing Materials

You may choose to generate other written marketing materials to provide to potential clients, such as a brochure or a one–page description of your firm's capabilities. Chapter 12 discusses when and how to provide written materials to potential clients to answer questions, provide food for thought, and to leave a tangible reminder of a meeting. Innovative lawyers and law firms create written materials that assist clients without crossing the line into providing legal advice. Ask yourself: What kinds of documents would be helpful for your potential clients and for referral sources? What information does someone need to have to hire you or to refer a friend or colleague to you? How can you help potential clients self–qualify and help referral sources qualify the people they know who could be potential clients? Answering these questions will help you determine what kinds of written materials you should create.

If you develop a collection of written materials to provide to your contacts, make certain that you also create an attractive folder to hold those materials together. The folder should be fairly simple, in colors that match your firm logo (if any) and with the firm's name and contact information imprinted onto the folder. One approach that is especially useful is to purchase two–pocket folders so that you can put substantive information (articles, for example) in the right–hand pocket and information about the firm (a one–page description of the firm with contact information, plus biographical sketches for relevant lawyers and staff) in the left–hand pocket.

Although some time may be required to generate or refine the written materials discussed in this chapter, you will find it helpful to spend that time creating these materials before you need them. These materials create a foundation for your rainmaking activity, because you will find it helpful for every other activity to have them ready at hand. The written materials that potential clients and referral sources review also contribute to the development of your "brand" and even your reputation as a lawyer.

The Bottom Line for Reluctant Rainmakers

Written marketing materials are your calling card when you meet a contact in person, by referral, or via the Internet. Having up–to–date materials that are easily accessible and informative will cast you and your practice in a positive light. These materials are especially useful for reluctant rainmakers because when you have strong written materials, you can focus your attention on the person with whom you are talking and leave behind written materials that detail your experience and expertise. When all written materials are coordinated in look and feel and are updated regularly, those materials represent you well and will deliver added comfort to contacts who may be considering hiring you or referring someone to you.

PART II

The Rainmaker's Toolkit

Introduction

Now that you have created or refined your business development plan and drafted strong written marketing materials, you are ready to take a deep look at the tactics you may employ to achieve your goals. A word of warning: choose just a few tactics at a time, generally no more than five, so that you can invest fully in each and determine to what extent each will be useful to you. If you decide to implement all of the suggested tactics, you will spread yourself too thin to see meaningful results for any of them, and your time will be wasted. Instead, review the tactics and select those that you consider most likely to be effective quickly, based on your objectives.

Rainmaking activities are generally divisible into two categories, though some tactics do straddle both. The first category is skills and credibility enhancement. To build the reputation of someone who has significant expertise in your field, you must not only engage in the activities that will actually build that expertise but also use some form of public outreach, such as writing or speaking, so that your name gets in circulation as someone knowledgeable in the field. These activities also provide credibility on your biographical sketch.

The second category into which business development activities fall is relationship–building. The most obvious of these tactics is networking (both in person and online); other examples include conducting client site visits, producing newsletters, and offering seminars to groups of "warm contacts." The hallmark of relationship–building activities is the opportunity to create a one–to–one connection, so that your contacts' experience with you deepens and they have a chance to come to know, like, and trust you.

As you probably already appreciate, some activities cross these two categories either innately or as a result of your approach to the activity. Teaching is probably the most obvious. When you teach, you are accorded the role of expert and obtain a credential to add to your biographical sketch. You also have an opportunity to use your time to build a relationship by inviting questions during breaks, by socializing with attendees during breaks, and perhaps by following up with attendees after the program. You are not required to engage in the relationship–building aspects of teaching, but if you are presenting to a group of people in your target audience, why would you choose not to do so?

The rainmaker's toolkit may also be separated by the likelihood and speed of yielding business. One–on–one, focused conversation with a current or former client is the highest yield activity, because you have already built a relationship, you have knowledge about the client and her legal needs, and (assuming you provided good technical work and good client service) you are more likely to be hired again by someone who already knows you than by a stranger. In contrast, article writing is a "slow yield" activity. It is a mistake to view it as low yield, because it so effectively establishes credibility and it can serve as the basis for creating a relationship or may be used to further an existing relationship. However, these results take time.

Part II, The Rainmaker's Toolkit, begins with a discussion of how to determine the likely payoff of an activity and then moves into the nuts and bolts of each tactic you might implement. Please be sure to review this section with your business development plan nearby. Your plan defines your objectives and will guide your approach. Without a strategy in place, you will find it difficult to know which activities are most likely to get you the results you seek. Even more challenging, you will be unable to evaluate the success of any activity without reference to a plan that sets out your goals and objectives. So, keep your plan close, develop a list of tactics that you would like to implement, and then choose a small number with which to begin.

Chapter 5

Invest in High–Yield Activities

One of the first objections lawyers lodge about rainmaking is that it draws time away from billable matters and from rare, precious, personal time. To handle this objection, we must first set aside the fact that, without business development, there would be no clients and thus no billable hours. That proposition is inarguable but unavailing for stressed, busy lawyers who genuinely cannot see how to clear enough time to take on rainmaking activities. Instead of looking at the "cost" of rainmaking time, look at the benefits it can deliver if used wisely. As soon as you decide that business development is important for your professional success and satisfaction, your mindset must shift to asking how to create the time even in

> *"Time stays for anyone who will use it."*
>
> *~Leonardo da Vinci*

your busy schedule. The critical element of time–effective business development is ensuring that you use your time wisely, by setting appropriate standards, priorities, and systems for the activities in which you participate. Time management strategies also create additional rainmaker action time, as discussed in Part IV.

Estimate the Investment/Payoff Ratio

Before engaging in any rainmaking activity, you must determine the investment–to–payoff ratio. Simply put, what results will your investment of time and energy buy you? Is there another activity that likely has a better yield? Your goal is to determine whether a given activity is likely to move you enough closer to your rainmaking goals to justify the activity's expense in time, energy, and money, recognizing that your estimate is only an estimate.

For instance, if you discover that networking with a particular industry organization yields numerous follow–up meetings and that 20% of those meetings yield client engagements and referrals with an average value of $19,000 within a year, that is a valuable activity[1]. You know, with reasonable certainty, that each time you have a one–hour lunch meeting with someone, there's a 20% chance that you'll make $19,000 within the year. Each meeting (plus follow–up, which might include a second

---

[1] Note that this is only an example and not an indication that you should get business from 20% of your contacts. Many factors go into how many contacts are required to yield new work, and as a rule of thumb, you will likely get new business more frequently if your average matter value is smaller and a less frequently if your average matter value is larger.

and maybe a third lunch meeting) is valued at approximately $3800 (20% of $19,000). In contrast, imagine that networking with another group yields a handful of follow–up meetings and that those meetings generate engagements and referrals within a year valued at $12,000 only 5% of the time. Each meeting, plus follow–up, in this instance is worth only $600. Given a choice, which meetings would you continue?

The figures and mathematical calculations used in this example are solely for illustrative purposes. To perform a similar calculation would require a great deal of certainty and precision. In addition, making these calculations requires a great deal of experience with the activity in question. If you are considering attending meetings of a new organization, you will be unable to calculate value with the specificity of the previous example. Likewise, until you have a track record with an activity, it will be difficult to judge its value. To enable yourself to estimate the value of your activities in this manner, you must maintain records of the time you spend in various activities as well as the results you achieve over time.

Use your time wisely, by setting standards, priorities, and systems for the activities in which you participate.

In addition, the value of the activity also depends on the goals you set for it. If you are a junior associate staffed on multi–million dollar deals, you are unlikely to land new business at this stage of your career. Your business development goals must be different from those of a senior partner handling the same kinds of matters. While your time may be well–spent in writing articles that will enhance your credibility in and your knowledge of your practice area, that time would likely be ineffective for the senior partner.

During the first few months and perhaps even years in which you run this kind of approximation, you will lack the information needed to make an accurate estimate. Your ability to predict your results will improve as time passes and you gain experience. Regardless of the accuracy of your estimation, though, simply considering what the result/investment ratio might be (even if you can reach only a qualitative, not a quantitative, estimate) will help you to make better decisions about how to use your time. Although each business development plan is unique, the most successful plans tend to have a distribution of high, medium, and low result/investment ratios. High–yield activities tend to indicate low–hanging fruit, meaning opportunities that will likely result in new business reasonably certainly and reasonably quickly. Medium–yield activities are more uncertain and take longer to show good results, and low–yield activities tend to be experimental or subject to removal from your list.

Some general guidelines are useful here:

- **Activities with clients are the most valuable activities you can do.** Whenever you have contact with a client, you have an opportunity to engage in business development. Your client already knows and, one would hope, likes and trusts you. The more you can do to develop that relationship through excellent client service and perhaps business/social activity, the more likely you are to retain that client's business and to receive more business and referrals from that client.

- **Activities with "warm contacts"** (those with whom you already have some relationship) have a higher yield than activities with strangers. As discussed in Chapter 2, if all other things are equal, people prefer to do business with those they know, like, and trust. Developing relationships with others and enhancing the "know, like, and trust" factors tends to be more valuable than one–time meetings with complete strangers.

- **Writing and speaking tend to be time–intensive activities with low immediate payoff.** The benefit of these activities lies in the credibility enhancement that follows. It is rare that an engagement or referral will follow directly from either of these activities, absent some personal contact between the lawyer and the client or referral source. If you are looking to generate business quickly, writing and speaking rank as a low–yield activity. If, however, your goal is to enhance your credentials, writing and speaking can be high–yield activities. As always, your objectives determine the likelihood of gain from any activity.

- **One–to–one relationship-building activity generally has a higher value yield than one–to–many activity.** Calculating the value of a group networking meeting almost certainly reveals a per–hour value that is considerably lower than the per–hour value of one–on–one follow–up meetings. If you attend a large group meeting and neglect to arrange follow–up meetings with the people you meet, the group meeting is effectively a waste of time unless it serves some other purpose, such as becoming known in your legal community.

- **Group participation is more valuable if you hold a leadership position.** As you will learn in Chapter 12, networking with individuals is useful only if you do the necessary follow–up, because without that follow-up, you are unlikely to build a relationship or make a memorable impression that will lead to business. If you hold a leadership role in an organization, however, you will become known to many more people than if you are simply a member. You will benefit significantly from holding a leadership role, especially if you are in a role that puts your name and, better yet, you in front of those who are in your target audience.
- **Sometimes an activity's value cannot be measured in purely financial terms.** For example, a client may request that you speak at a conference, and doing so would be a favor to that client. While you are unlikely to see any financial value directly traced to delivering the favor and the presentation, the client's gratitude may be equally valuable. In this instance, you might also consider whether you could recruit someone else who would be a better match for the client's request. Done properly, that substitution could save you time, offer a benefit to your substitute, and still earn the client's appreciation.

Look at your business development plan and begin making an estimate of the result/investment value of each activity that you have planned to incorporate. If you lack the data to make even a rudimentary mathematical calculation, make a qualitative estimate using the system of high, medium, and low result/investment ratios.

If a substantial proportion of activities in your plan ranks low, you should re–evaluate to be sure that you have estimated the ratio accurately: ask whether you have given the appropriate weight to credential– and foundation–building activities, for instance. If your estimates are reasonable, select some of the low–ranking activities and look for ways to replace them with higher value activities. It is unlikely that you will be able to craft a business development plan that includes only high–yield activities, and it is inadvisable to craft a business plan that includes only low–yield activities. Work with your mentor, rainmaker group, or coach to tweak your plan so that you have an effective mix.

In addition to evaluating the plans that you set for their result/investment ratio, train yourself to make an estimate before accepting any request. The more senior and the more successful you become in your practice, the more likely you will receive requests to speak and write or to attend certain groups. Make it your habit to build in evaluation time before you respond to any such invitation. As noted previously, you may reap non–financial rewards that make otherwise low–yield activities worthwhile, but you must recognize unprofitable activities quickly and substitute something more likely to garner the results that you seek.

Act According to Your Priorities

Prioritization is a key aspect of any time management attempt, and rainmaking efforts are no different. Chapter 2 discussed the priorities that you should apply for business development purposes:

1. **Current clients**
2. **Former clients and referral sources**
3. **"Warm" potential clients and referral sources**
4. **Strangers**

As you move into business development activity, keep these priorities at the forefront of your mind and ensure that your mix of rainmaking tasks reflects them. If time demands that you drop some of your planned activities, make sure you drop the ones that rank lowest on this priority scale.

Remember too that you have business development opportunities with your current clients every time you perform work for them. The skill and service you offer in the course of your representations will serve to develop relationships, as will the casual conversation that occurs in the course of the engagements. Every lawyer will experience times in which business development activity has to take a backseat to other demands, whether it is an enormous and pressing client project or a difficult personal situation. During those times, look to your billable work as client development, and focus your attention on making every effort count.

Create Rainmaking Systems

Business development activity is, by its nature, unique to each person and each opportunity you encounter. You cannot design a routine for meeting members of an organization you join and follow it without deviation while expecting to realize the same results that you achieve when you adjust your approach based on the people you meet, the conversations you have, and the opportunities that present themselves. You will get better results if you enter each activity with a strategy and with the intent to change and adapt it as necessary. But you can create systems for following up with the people you meet while networking and for repurposing written material (write an article, for instance, then turn an excerpt into a blog post, revise it as material for your newsletter, and use social media to announce each publication).

> ***Develop the habit of looking for ways to systematize common activities.***

Each subsequent chapter discusses specific ways that you can design systems to make your rainmaking life simpler. Beyond those suggestions, though, develop the habit of looking for ways to systematize common activities. For instance, if you decide to recognize your clients' birthdays and anniversaries, set up a system so that your assistant checks the dates at the beginning of the month and prepares cards for you to sign in bulk. If you choose to call acquaintances when your travel takes you to their cities, devise a system to ensure that your assistant sorts through your database at least a week before your trip to generate a list of area contacts.

The systems you devise will be unique to your business development plan and your preferred mode of operation. To make maximum use of your time, be sure that you are constantly watching for repetitive activities that could be systematized. Check with your mentor, coach, or rainmaking group to see what systems they use, which will keep you from reinventing the wheel.

The Bottom Line for Reluctant Rainmakers

You will find it difficult to commit the time and energy to carry out your business development plans if you do not see results to justify your work. This general principle is even more applicable for those who do not enjoy the tasks at hand, as is the case for reluctant rainmakers who have not yet received a benefit from their endeavors. You must avoid the trap of self-perpetuated failure, in which a lawyer undertakes some activity but, not seeing fantastic results immediately, concludes that the activity is pointless and that she can never be a rainmaker. The best way to avoid this trap is to invest in high-yield activities and to make sure your objectives are clear and reasonable. By spending your time on activities that are likely to garner the results you want, you create opportunities for success. Over time, you will build on each success and see steadily increasing rainmaking results. Nothing overcomes reluctance in rainmaking like success.

Chapter 6

Writing and Speaking

Writing and speaking are two of the most important credential– and credibility–enhancing activities in which you can engage. This chapter addresses the two together because most of the principles apply equally to these two forms of public communication, although certain differences will be highlighted. Both speaking and writing afford you opportunities to get your name in front of your colleagues, potential clients, and referral resources.

As discussed earlier, many lawyers expect that they will be able to attract clients simply by virtue of their excellent legal skill, but that expectation is almost always incorrect. It is true that a few lawyers are so highly skilled that clients seek them out in the absence of any relationship, solely on the basis of their reputation. However, some communication is necessary for people to become aware of these select lawyers, and that communication typically occurs through writings and speeches by or about the lawyer. These lawyers' work forms the foundation of their reputation, which is then enhanced and extended by their writings and speeches. Even the most highly skilled lawyers must be known for their abilities before they are retained; otherwise, their skills would go unused in the quiet of an office without clients. The same is true for practitioners of more ordinary reputation, known to possess strong but not genius–level legal abilities, whose practices are built on relationships with clients and referral sources. If you are not known to others, you will not have clients.

Every lawyer must begin somewhere in building a reputation, and writing and speaking form a solid foundation for that effort. Having reasonable legal competency is a prerequisite for client engagements, and legal adequacy will usually be assumed in the absence of evidence to the contrary. Most clients want to find a lawyer with better than adequate legal skills, but most clients are unable to identify the line between adequate and superior skills. Reputation enters here. If a potential client is unable to judge objectively the level of legal skill possessed by a lawyer he is considering hiring, he will look instead to the lawyer's reputation. Is she known to be bright, creative, and ethical? Often, reputation will be shared via personal referral. When no referral is available, though, or when a potential client must choose whom to contact from several referrals, he will probably look at the candidate lawyers' biographical sketches to review their credentials, and he will then make some judgment about the lawyers' skill based on those credentials. Clients look to lawyers' actual expertise and

> ***Speaking and writing afford you opportunities to get your name in front of your colleagues, potential clients, and referral sources.***

their reputation for skill in the legal field in which the client needs assistance.

Writing and speaking serve both to develop or to enhance your actual expertise and to create credentials that support others' perception of your expertise. If you have ever written an article or prepared a presentation that deals with some aspect of law, you probably know firsthand that there is no way to learn the law like teaching it to someone else. Writing an article or delivering a lecture on some specific aspect of your practice will require you to do some research, perhaps reading recent cases or law review articles, bringing you up to date with the most recent developments in that area. The process of developing your material and making it comprehensible to others will develop your familiarity with and understanding of the topic of your article or presentation. It will help to enhance your technical skills in that area, and it will certainly enhance your knowledge of the current state of the law.

You must be able to measure your results and to know, before you begin, what results would make it worthwhile for you to write an article or make a speech.

Moreover, speaking and writing will develop your reputation as an expert[2] by increasing others' perception of your skill. When someone is a speaker or a published author in any field, she is expected to have the knowledge

---

[2] Be aware that most jurisdictions restrict the use of the word "expert" and "expertise." As always, know the applicable ethical rules.

necessary to do a good job of presenting the material. As an author, when your name appears on an article in a bar journal or an industry journal, you are further enhancing the perception of your expertise, and those who read your work will likely see you as someone who knows your topic well. The same is true for speakers. Of course, those expectations may be shattered if you lack the necessary knowledge about your field, but few lawyers will offer a manuscript or step onto a dais without ensuring that they know enough to make a strong showing. Speaking and writing are, therefore, two of the best ways to enhance your credentials and your credibility in your field of practice.

Preliminary Considerations

Before you agree to speak or to write an article, you must ask yourself several questions to make sure your time will be well invested. Writing and speaking both require a substantial investment of your time to develop a good final product, and you must perform some due diligence to ensure that the final result is likely to merit the necessary investment of time and energy. Ask yourself the following questions:

- **Is this the right audience?** Consider the correct venue to reach your target audience. For example, if your clients and referral sources are generally not lawyers, writing an article for a bar association journal will not serve your purposes. If you want to get your name in front of general counsel and upper level management for technology companies, for example, you might choose to speak to a meeting of the Licensing Executive Society, which is often attended by people in those two groups. If you are planning to write an article, be sure that contacts whom you want to reach read the journal in which you intend to publish. If you plan to speak, be sure that those contacts attend the meeting where you plan to lecture. Writing and speaking to the wrong audience (that is, an audience composed of people whom you do not serve or people who are not in a position to refer potential clients to you) will not generate enough benefit to justify the investment of time, so answer this foundational question before you consider or do anything else.

- **How much time will this require?** Writing a short, practical article will require much less of a time investment than writing a full–length law review article. Similarly, serving on a panel will typically take less preparation time than presenting a ninety–minute speech by yourself. How much time will the contemplated activity require? Without this information, you will be unable to calculate the expected result/investment ratio. If you are practicing in a larger firm, you will find that the amount of time you must invest to engage in writing and speaking drops as you become more senior and can call for assistance from others, such as a junior associate or a non–competitive sole practitioner colleague. Unless and until you can call on such support, however, you may find that larger projects are unmanageable or must be relegated to long–term projects status.

- **What results would make the expenditure of time**

worthwhile? You must be able to measure your results and to know, before you begin, what results would make it worthwhile for you to have written this article or made this speech. If your goal is simply to add a credential to your biographical sketch, any writing or speaking is likely to accomplish that objective. If, however, you want to speak to an audience composed primarily of in-house counsel, that objective will necessarily define the scope of opportunities that you would consider. Be sure to keep your eye on your objectives and do not allow yourself to be seduced by entreaties to help a colleague who is searching for someone to serve as an author or speaker. You must know what results you want to achieve, and you must be able to predict (with some reason to expect the accuracy of the prediction) that the activity you plan will produce those results.

- **How does this activity—the writing or speaking—compare to more immediately high-yield activity?** Regardless of how terrific your presentation or your article is, and regardless of the subject matter and the kind of results that you achieve, speaking and writing both tend to be relatively *slow-yield* opportunities. Slow-yield should not be confused with low-yield activities, but you also must not expect to see immediate business-generation results. Because you are typically developing your expertise and the perception of your expertise, and because both speaking and writing tend to require a substantial time investment, fast results beyond credential-enhancement are improbable.

It is highly unlikely that you will write an article, get it published, and have your phone ring with a potential client calling you because she saw that article. (If your practice is sufficiently niched, however, you might be like my patent attorney client who built his practice by publishing a series of articles for inventors in a foreign language newspaper.) More likely, you will write an article or make a speech that will broadcast your name in several different ways, and you will show up in enough places addressing some particular aspect of the law that a potential client or a referral source will call you because he has come to see you as an expert. Repeated exposure creates the perception of expertise. You should not expect to write or speak once and then receive a call that leads directly to an engagement.

Because writing and speaking are slow–yield activities, you must consider whether you would be better advised to invest your time in something that is a higher–yield activity. For instance, if you have a choice between writing an article or going to a current client's office for a meeting to discuss a potential expansion of your engagement, the client meeting will be more likely to generate new billable work 100% of the time. Even a meeting with a current client to discuss something other than new work is more likely to yield new business than writing an article or making a speech in most instances. Would it be a better investment of time to have lunch with a referral source or a contact who has been asking you questions that suggest she may have a legal need within your area of practice? Sometimes the question is difficult to answer, but you must consider it and make an evaluation of the benefit of doing this activity versus doing others.

I once coached a lawyer who had numerous articles to her credit. An excellent writer who was uncomfortable attending meetings for networking, she decided early in her career that writing would be her primary business development activity. She discovered that although her articles impressed contacts, they rarely initiated the next step to call her and discuss hiring her. Through our work together, she identified several ways to combine her love for writing with working directly with those in a position to hire her, such as serving on a report–drafting committee in the organization to which many of her potential clients belonged. She soon began receiving inquiries that led to new business. One new client told her that he had read her articles over the years, and she asked him what prompted him to discuss working with her after such a long time. Imagine her astonishment when he responded that he had always assumed that she was too busy and too much of an expert to take on new work! Meeting and working with her created an opportunity that probably would not have occurred otherwise.

Writing and Speaking to Get Results

When you decide that you are going to speak or write, you need to know what to do to garner business from that activity. Most importantly, you must develop the speech or article from the ideal client's point of view. The person reading your article or listening to your presentation (your ideal client or referral source) must understand immediately how your comments apply to him.

For example, if your ideal client profile includes small business owners with annual revenue in the range of $350,000, you might write an article that explicitly identifies the target readers and addresses the decision of whether to have a trademark registered to cover proprietary systems used in those businesses. A reader would know whether she matches the client described (thus self–qualifying as a potential client or disqualifying) and will be drawn into the article if she has been mulling over trademark registration. Such a reader will receive benefit from an article that sets out the factors to consider, and she will know immediately that you are someone who could help her with that decision and with the registration process should she decide to move forward. A practical article with tips for guidance will be much more useful for that potential client than a law–review style article that begins by discussing what trademarks are, how they came to exist, how they are prosecuted, and how long trademark protection applies.

You must develop the speech or article from your ideal client's point of view.

In most instances, a problem–and–solution presentation will be more likely to draw in and to benefit your potential clients and referral sources than an academic presentation. They will find useful information, and they will also identify themselves as the kind of client you are describing. So, in writing and in speaking, you should move fairly quickly through historical background and context and get practical very quickly.

Consider the marketing truism that, "Facts tell, stories sell." To continue the previous example, if you write an article about how to go through the process of filing a trademark application, that a trademark will be in force for a certain period of time, that the owner must renew the mark periodically, and so on, the reader may find the information interesting and perhaps useful in some ways. That information will not educate her about whether she needs to have her mark registered (and will not even pique the reader's curiosity about whether you are the lawyer who might help register her mark) because the dry explanation will not connect with her.

Instead, tell a story about a client who gave some thought to the marks he was considering, then hired you to look at common law protection and state and federal law registration and to analyze what each would do under the circumstances. Describe the factors you recommended the client consider in his decision to register the mark. This approach will allow a potential client to put herself immediately in that client's position and to apply what the article is explaining to her business. That story–focused presentation will be much more persuasive than simply telling the potential client the facts that she must assimilate and think through.

In preparing stories for articles or presentations, you may consider featuring your clients, if they will give their permission, or simply creating case studies based on composite clients. By doing so, you also seed the idea that you helped the client you describe with his legal needs, creating the subtextual impression that you could help the reader or listener as well.

When you structure your article or presentation, you must first present the business problem. What is the issue that is causing a problem to the person reading your article? What is the pain? Then tell a story about someone who was in the same kind of situation. Describe what that person or organization experienced, using both facts and emotional words so that your audience or readers or listeners recognize themselves in the story and identify with the story. Next, outline the solutions. How did you help? You can present the legal answer and the approach to the problem so that the reader or listener understands what needed to be done in the story.

Finally, close your article or presentation by telling the reader or listener (whom you should now regard as the potential client or referral source) what he needs to do. What are the next steps? In marketing language, this is a call to action. If you want the reader to contact you, you must give him a reason to do so. You might offer a resource, such as a checklist, another article that will help in addressing the problem, or a consultation. This is an ideal time to offer a subscription to your newsletter, which offers additional information pertinent to the reader's interests. (See Chapter 13 for further discussion of launching and operating a newsletter for your contacts.)

> ***Facts tell, stories sell.***

You must consider the applicable ethics rules when deciding how to phrase your call to action, but it is essential to give some reason to contact you and to get into further conversation if you hope to generate business from your work. If your goal is solely to enhance your credentials, however, the call to action is less important.

As you prepare your article or presentation, make sure that you are using the appropriate language. If you are writing to lawyers, you will likely use legal terms and jargon, but you should omit all jargon when you write or speak to non–lawyers who may not be legally sophisticated. Your audience should not have to work too hard to discern what you are trying to explain, whether and why it is relevant to them, or what they should take from your article or your presentation. The harder more that readers need to work to understand your presentation, the less likely they will be inclined to view you as the expert who can shepherd them through their problems. Tailor your comments to your readers' level of understanding and to their level of interest.

About Article Writing

Good news about article writing: practical articles almost always outperform academic articles for business purposes. Practical articles, defined as those that focus on describing the situation, the legal issues, the considerations, and potential solutions, are typically more useful to clients and to referral sources. Instead of going back into legal history to trace the development of the current law and looking forward to forecast what the law should be, practical articles limit their inquiry to the state of the law right now. Practical articles tell potential clients what they need to do and what they should be thinking about. Easier to write than law review articles, which require full footnote citation, practical articles may be as bare–bones as a description of a problem and a bullet–point list of factors that readers should consider.

Practical articles build the perception of your expertise and tell potential clients what course of action you might recommend, although you should also include disclaimer language to remind the reader that every situation carries wrinkles that may impact the analysis and direction of the matter. If you close with a call to action, readers will know whether they are in the group of people toward whom your article was directed, they will have some ability to evaluate your recommended approach, they will recognize that you may be able to help them with their legal needs, and they will know how to contact you. A practical article can be extremely helpful to a properly selected audience.

> ***Practical articles almost always outperform academic articles for business purposes.***

By the same token, shorter articles typically outperform long articles for business development purposes. Shorter articles tend to be easier to write, especially if the approach is practical rather than academic and they may be easier to get published. Finally, given the limited time available and shrinking attention span that now affects so many readers, short articles are more likely to be read in full than a long article.

Although law review articles may offer substantial credential enhancement (and are effectively required for certain practice areas), shorter, more practical articles will probably be better suited for rainmaking purposes.

Repurposing Material

Once you complete an article or are slated to make a presentation, what do you do next? Given the limited time that most lawyers have available for writing and speaking, you absolutely must ensure that you repurpose your work product. A client I worked with was a prolific author and frequent speaker, and early in our coaching together I asked how he reused his work product. After a moment's silence, he responded that he had never given thought to reusing material, and that once he had written an article or made a presentation, he considered it done and not to be revisited. Patrick was careful to target his work well and to ensure that he would a get good return on his investment in writing and speaking, so his time certainly was not wasted, but neglecting to repurpose article and presentation materials is a lost opportunity. I recommend that you write once (whether the once is an article or your outline for an oral presentation) and then rework that material into at least three other forms.

For instance, if you have written a 2500–word article, consider reworking it as a client newsletter article or legal alert (perhaps by shortening it, changing the language around, and removing legal terms of art), turning it into a blog post or a series of posts (see Chapter 7), and reading an excerpt from the article to create a podcast. In addition, you could submit your articles to an online article database, which is a clearinghouse that matches written content with blog and online newsletter publishers in need of that content.

> ***Always rework your content into at least three other forms.***

Article databases typically have particular categories, such as law or subtopics within an umbrella of the legal category. Publishers may use articles submitted to these directories on the condition that they include the author's full contact information (known as a "resource box," which may include links to your website) and that they do not edit the article in any way. Permitting your articles to be republished creates an opportunity to get your name in circulation. Having articles republished on the Internet also creates opportunities for your article and name to turn up in an online search and may improve your search engine ranking as your articles link back to your website.

Publicize Your Material

When you are engaged in article writing or in speaking, consider how to publicize your speeches and your articles to current clients, former clients, perspective clients, referral sources, and any other friends of your practice. For instance, if you are speaking at a CLE meeting, you might want to invite a select number of your clients or former clients to attend the presentation. Share a copy of an article with contacts who have some interest in the subject matter, either by sending it directly to your contact with a cover note or by publishing it in your own newsletter.

You should consider posting at least a reference to your presentations and your articles on your website. An even more effective strategy is to upload the article or a summary of your presentation to your website. Having content–rich information on your website, especially when that information includes or is described by relevant keywords, may increase your search engine rankings. This strategy is essentially the first–grade version of search engine optimization and is by no means an ultimate search engine optimization strategy. However, it does offer some search engine self–help and permits you to get the maximum benefit of your articles and presentations.

If you are active in social media, such as LinkedIn, Twitter, Google+, or Facebook, you may link your article or an announcement of your presentation to your profile there. You could post a status saying, "Article just published on [topic]. Check it out here," and include the URL of the website page where your article is located. You might also consider posting your articles or summaries of your presentations to lawyer–specific social media sites such as JD Supra. (See Chapter 14 for more information about using social media.)

Placing your articles and presentations online can be highly effective in raising your ranking in online searches. Imagine that a potential client plugs your name and an area of the law into Google and finds your website listed high in the results, perhaps as a function of full–fledged search engine optimization and assisted by several of your articles or a blog on your website. Imagine further if the searcher finds your articles published in someone else's newsletter, links from social media, and other references with your name. If a potential client who has received your name through a referral source or who has located your name through her own homework types your name into Google and finds information about you and publications by you, she will likely regard you as an expert in your field. You will hold substantial credibility with that potential client.

Posting your articles and speeches online can be highly effective in increasing the perception of your expertise.

Using Articles for Networking Follow–up

You will see in Chapter 12 that networking is wasted without appropriate follow–up. When you write articles and make presentations, you create content for your networking follow–up contacts. One strong way to enhance relationships is to deliver some sort of follow–up material that is useful for the person with whom you are building a relationship. If you have an article, or if you can issue an invitation to a speaking event, you have valuable follow–up content to deliver. It may be helpful information for your contact, and because you are the author or speaker, you are positioned as the expert.

When you offer you own article or presentation, you provide a useful resource and you subtly increase the perception of your expertise. You are the person who wrote the article or made the presentation, which implies that you are knowledgeable enough and sufficiently well–regarded in the field to have been invited to publish or to participate. Better yet, you are available to answer you contact's questions or to give further explanation or direction.

Summary and Assignment

Be strategic about your speaking and writing activities. Be thoughtful about where you choose to engage. Be sure each opportunity you choose is a good investment of your time. Make sure you are getting the maximum possible value from your efforts by repurposing what you have done. Get your articles and presentations in front of your clients, your former clients, your potential clients, your referral sources, and any contacts who might be interested.

Here is your coaching assignment: identify some appropriate speaking and writing opportunities for yourself. Look at the purpose, the audience, the topic, and look at the timing. Select one or two opportunities that you would like to develop within the next six to eight months. Make sure you identify specific goals and desired consequences so that after you have completed the article or the presentation you can look back and see whether you achieved the results you had wanted. Finally, before you get started writing or preparing your oral presentation, decide how you are going to repurpose your material.

The Bottom Line for Reluctant Rainmakers

Writing and speaking can be excellent business development activities if you use them appropriately. Make sure these activities meet your objectives well, especially in view of the amount of time you will be required to invest. Get your articles or presentations in front of the appropriate people, cast your comments in an action–oriented way that paints the problem and solution, and offer a reason for readers or listeners to contact you. Do not, however, rely on writing or speaking without person–to–person contact with your contacts that may hire you or refer others to you.

Chapter 7

Blogging

Blogging is a special subcategory of writing that has attained significant attention over the last few years. A weblog, now almost always called by the shortened title "blog," is an online journal in which entries are published by date and generally tagged as to topic and/or category. The entries, called posts, are usually shorter and less formal than articles that would appear in a newsletter or other journal. To reap the maximum benefit of blogging, new posts should be published at least weekly (and preferably two to three times a week), on a consistent basis. Frequent publication tends to generate growing and consistent readership, and those readers often have the chance to comment on posts. Comments and responses that turn into conversation and build relationships (whether on the blog itself or on the social media platform where posts are shared) are a hallmark of a blog and the key point that distinguishes a blog post from an article.

Blogging initially gained a reputation as an online diary in which blog authors (known as bloggers) could detail their daily lives, down to what they had for breakfast and their innermost thoughts. Although those kinds of blogs do still exist, they are not at all useful for business development or for reputation enhancement. A legally–oriented blog (sometimes called a "blawg") that centers on your area of practice, however, may offer several advantages. First, as a form of social media, blogs can create ongoing conversations with other bloggers, many of whom will be other practitioners. You can develop relationships through these contacts, which may in turn lead to invitations to write or speak, referrals, and perhaps even co–counsel relationships.

Second, by writing posts on a regular basis that address some aspect of your practice area, you have the chance to showcase your expertise and develop your reputation as an influential lawyer in the field. Perhaps the best example of someone who used blogging to establish a high professional profile is Dennis Crouch, the author of the Patently–O blog. (You may visit the blog at http://www.patentlyo.com/.) Crouch began his blog, which reviews every Federal Circuit decision on matters of patent law, in his first year in practice. His blog quickly became the preeminent blog for patent law.

As a result of blogging, Crouch generated speaking invitations, book deals, and thousands of devoted readers, plus new client engagements. Crouch noted that in two years the blog generated "less than $1 million" of business for his firm, an amount that would leave most junior associates at the edge of joyous delirium. After four years in practice, Crouch became an associate professor of law at the University of Missouri Law School, where he continues to write Patently–O. Admittedly, very few bloggers could hope for the success that Crouch has experienced, but his story indicates that blogs have nearly unlimited potential for reputation building that leads to great opportunity.

Because bloggers write on topics of interest to those in their own practice areas, either as colleagues in law or as potential clients, the posts naturally tend to be content– and keyword–rich. As a result, search engines pick up on the posts quickly, and blog posts can vault to the top of search engine results. Similarly, the social nature of blogging calls for cross–links among posts on various authors' blogs, and those links can prove to be valuable for search engine purposes as well because links from other websites indicate to the search engines that the site at issue is likely to be useful to its users. As discussed *infra* in Chapter 14, Google+ now offers significant search engine advantages to those who blog.

> ***Because blog posts are designed to educate, you place yourself in the role of expert, delivering useful content to your readers in a conversational way that communicates something about yourself and your approach to practice.***

Blogging also creates the opportunity to grow actual expertise, perhaps even more quickly than ordinary article–writing. Little benefit accrues to those who draft ill–considered posts: other bloggers may critique posts that lack substantive value, and readers will be unlikely to return. However, if you spend time finding issues of interest to potential clients who may find your blog, and you do a credible job of discussing those topics, you will build the related expertise and, potentially, a reputation as a go–to source for information.

Even more importantly, because blog posts are designed to educate, you will place yourself in the role of expert, and you will deliver useful content to your readers in a conversational way that also communicates something about yourself and your approach to practice. Current and potential clients will receive helpful information and will come to know you better, which offers the potential for significant return on investment. Journalists now routinely search blogs to find sources, and study after study reveals that clients frequently make hiring decisions at least in part based on reading a lawyer's blog.

Finally, although blogging may sound technically challenging, the truth is that maintaining a blog is as easy as drafting an e-mail. With a brief investment of time, you can get your message in front of thousands of clients and potential clients, you can develop potentially valuable relationships with other lawyer–bloggers ("blawggers"), and you can boost your profile as an authority in your field.

If you are considering blogging, invest some time in educating yourself about the blogosphere (the universe of blogs) and what makes a blog successful. The Rainmaker Resource List (http://www.TheReluctantRainmaker.com) includes links to blawg directories that you should review to find others who are writing in your area of interest. This initial research will allow you to make connections with those bloggers and to find something to distinguish your blog from others in the same field.

Spending time setting up your own blog is unlikely to be a good use of your time, unless you enjoy working with code, but for somewhere between a few hundred and a few thousand dollars you can hire someone who will create a blog that serves as a professional showpiece and communication tool. The Rainmaker Resource List (http://www.TheReluctantRainmaker.com) includes resources on blogging for lawyers. As you consider starting a blog, here are a few questions to guide you:

- **What area of practice will your blog address?** The most successful legal blogs focus on a narrow area of practice, whether based on the substantive topic or jurisdiction covered. If your blog is designed to appeal to everyone, it may be so loosely focused that it will instead appeal to no one. Select a single area and delve deeply into it.
- **Who will author your blog?** Some blogs have a single author, while others offer posts drafted by a group. Each has an advantage: if you are the sole author, you have complete authority over what goes onto the blog, how often you publish, what design elements to incorporate, and so on. If you blog with a group, however, you will be required to invest less time and you may still reap significant benefits. For business development purposes, be sure that any group you create is composed of non–competitive lawyers. If you work in a law firm, a natural group might be other firm lawyers in your same practice area. If you are a sole practitioner, perhaps you could create a group of solo lawyers who address different aspects of a single client's needs—for example, if the blog addresses single parents, you might have a group with a domestic lawyer, an estate planning lawyer, an education lawyer, and the like. (If you write with others, consider what will happen to the blog and to your contributions if you leave the firm or the authorship group.)

- **How often will you publish?** While frequency of posting may vary, establishing a regular schedule creates better marketing opportunities. Readers will know when to expect new material from you, and you will not be lulled into silence by delaying your next post until tomorrow and tomorrow and tomorrow. Frequent posting accrues significant benefit.
- **How will readers access your posts?** The most common way for readers to read blog posts, at least initially, is by going to the blog's website and reading them online. You will be able to serve (and market to) your readers more effectively if you "push" new posts to them, meaning that you create a system by which new posts are delivered to them by RSS feed or by e-mail. Several services exist to do just this, and you will find resources on the Rainmaker Resource List (http://www.TheReluctantRainmaker.com) or through the person or company who sets up your blog for you.
- **What tone will you use for your blog?** The Patently–O Blog has a reporter's voice. Although some posts include commentary, that blog's primary purpose is to inform readers about the Federal Circuit's decisions, developments that will affect patent law, and possible consequences. Other blogs offer more opinionated posts, and yet others present a mix of fact and commentary. You should also consider whether you want to be a "character" on your blog or simply an omniscient narrator. If you inject your personality into your posts (to a degree that fits the blog's overall tone) you will develop more of a relationship with your readers, which may be beneficial for rainmaking purposes.

- Will you allow comments? If so, what degree of comment author authentication will you require? While most legal blogs do not attract "trolls" whose sole purpose is to sow controversy and dissention, you would probably prefer not to offer a forum for an anonymous poster who could verbally attack you, your practice, your posts, and so on. Requesting an e-mail address (and validating that address before posting the comment) or assuming moderator control over all comments allows you to ensure that comments do not run awry from the blog's purpose. The person or company creating and maintaining your blogsite will be able to offer resources and recommendations on achieving the proper balance between free exchange of thought and appropriate oversight in comments. If you elect to restrict comments, however, you will lose the opportunity to build relationships through your writing.

Consider the benefit of blogging, survey other lawyers who blog in the area that you might address, and when you are armed with that knowledge, ask the critical question: is the likely result of blogging worth the necessary investment of time and money? As always, you might share your thoughts with your mentor, your rainmaker group, or your coach to get feedback. You could also ask current and former clients whether they would find the blog you are contemplating helpful. Blogging can yield astounding results, if properly used, but you should consider your commitment before you begin.

One concern that stops many lawyers from launching a blog is the fear of running out of content. What if you hit a publication day and find you have nothing to say? You can spark your creativity in many ways, but the surest insurance against this problem is to keep a file (preferably in Evernote or in some other format that you can access no matter where you are) with all of your topic ideas. When you have a long menu of topics, you will never be stuck with writer's block.

The Bottom Line for Reluctant Rainmakers

Blogging is a different kind of writing opportunity that carries potential benefits and challenges. The shorter posts of a legal blog generally require less time to write than a full–length article, and because the "blogosphere" operates as a community, bloggers may be able to parlay this writing opportunity into a networking opportunity. A writer must make a longer–term commitment to blogging than to article–writing. A blog that goes fallow reflects poorly on blogger, which may create unanticipated negative perceptions of his practice. Moreover, while some bloggers relish the challenge of finding blog–worthy news or opinions on a regular basis, others look on that added demand as a painful burden. Is blogging right for you? Consider the likely costs and benefits (including the statistics on clients who read blogs to identify counsel), but do not undertake blogging lightly.

Chapter 8

Teaching

Serving as an adjunct professor for a law school is an often-overlooked credibility– and credential–enhancing activity. The bar for moving into academia as a career is quite high: stellar grades from an outstanding law school, strong work experience, and a clerkship are usually considered to be prerequisites for law professors. Many schools, however, invite local practitioners to serve as adjunct professors for certain classes, generally including legal research and writing along with more specialized topics such as patent law. Such classes are usually scheduled once a week for a two–hour block in the late afternoon or evening.

Teaching a class is time–intensive, especially on your maiden voyage as an instructor. Although you will teach in your own area of specialty, and will therefore be at least familiar with the subjects you will present, you will need to put time into creating a lesson plan, devising your lecture, planning questions to prompt classroom discussion, and being available during limited office hours. You may also be required to grade final examinations or final papers, which is likely to require a substantial investment of time over just a few weeks. If you have a passion for teaching, that passion may tip the result/investment ratio enough to justify taking on a role as an adjunct professor. Otherwise, you should consider carefully what benefits might accrue as a result of your teaching and evaluate carefully whether serving as an adjunct professor is a good investment of your time and energy—recognizing especially that the pay that you could expect to receive will likely not approach fully compensation for the investment of time that you will be required to make.

What benefits might you realize as an instructor? Indulging a love for teaching is, as already noted, at the top of the list. You will likely augment your knowledge of your area of practice by focusing on the details of cases that you may not have reviewed in years, which can provide long–term payoffs as you deepen your appreciation for the micro–level view of the law in your area. Finally, teaching a law school class will unquestionably cast you as an authority in your field and will support others' perception of your skill, however that perception may have been developed. It is also possible that students who attend your class may eventually contact you with a request to serve as co–counsel or to make a referral to you, though you should discount that possibility when evaluating the potential benefits of this activity.

> ***If you take on a part–time academic assignment, be sure to consider how you can repurpose your work.***

Many colleges and graduate schools offer legally–focused classes such as "business law" and "patent law for engineers." Although the time investment is likely to be similar, you may find a greater chance of receiving business from or through a student in one of these classes than from a law student. The prestige factor is somewhat lower for non–law school teaching experiences, but you will nonetheless bolster your credentials by adding an academic appointment at any level.

If you choose to take on a part–time academic assignment, be sure to consider whether and how you might extend the work you do in teaching into other avenues. You might, for example, notice an interesting legal development that would be a good subject for a short article. If you teach a class of non–law students, you might develop ideas for practical articles that you could issue as legal alerts or blog posts, or you might be able to repurpose some of your lecture content into podcasts for your clients. Because the amount of time required to teach any course will be substantial, ensure that you have a plan to reap the maximum possible benefit from it.

Note that this section does not address the common tactic of offering a seminar or workshop to clients or potential clients invited by you or others in your referral network. See Chapter 11 for further discussion of this mode of teaching

The Bottom Line for Reluctant Rainmakers

Teaching at a law school or undergraduate institution can be an effective way to enhance your credentials and perhaps to garner referrals. It is, however, one of the most time–intensive activities you can undertake. Consider carefully whether the benefits you expect to receive from teaching outweigh the costs.

Chapter 9

Organizational Involvement

Almost every business development plan includes some organizational involvement. Many lawyers begin rainmaking activity by joining and becoming active in a local bar association. Others may explore the organizations in which their ideal clients congregate. The array of associations is almost mind-boggling, and with some research, you can probably find an organization that will allow you to share your expertise in a way that educates and attracts potential clients and is enjoyable to you. Volunteer work for an organization allows you to leverage your time and to know and become known by many people in less time than you would need to meet them one by one. For this reason alone, though others do exist, becoming involved in an appropriate organization is a good use of your time—assuming that you become active in an organization where your ideal clients, referral sources, or centers of influence gather.

When you think about becoming involved with an organization, you must first consider your objectives. Do you want to meet and mingle with potential clients? Or is your goal to develop a network of referral sources? Sometimes a single organization will yield both results, but more often your goals will dictate the kind of group that will be most beneficial for you.

Bar Association Involvement

In most jurisdictions lawyers must join the state bar for states in which they are licensed. As a result, bar association membership may be the most obvious target for organizational involvement. You should consider becoming active with a local, state, or national bar association for a variety of reasons:

- **To grow your professional network.** Having a broad group of colleagues will prove useful over the span of your career. Professional networks are useful if you need co–counsel on a case, if you are conflicted out and want to refer a client to someone in whom you have confidence, if you would like to take a deposition in an office in a distant city, and if you are searching for a new position—to name a few instances. Sole practitioners may find the collegial relationships that grow from bar association work to be particularly useful to form an affiliation of colleagues you can contact to bounce around an idea or to get fresh insight into a thorny problem you are facing with a client or in your practice.
- **To contribute to the profession.** Each bar group will produce varying amounts and types of work product. You may have an opportunity to

contribute to a report studying the challenges faced by women attorneys of color, the impact of multiple tiers of partners, or the latest revision to substantive or procedural rules of practice, for example, or you could write an article on a topic of interest to you and have it published to a narrow (or broad) audience of lawyers. You can use your skills and develop them further through this work, and you can build a reputation for your knowledge as well as for the way you approach practice.

- **To contribute to society in general.** Some groups will focus on work that directly impacts individuals, such as writing a report and passing a policy supporting or objecting to proposals relating to privacy, public health, and more. Although bar associations do not have lawmaking authority, some have quite a bit of clout. You could potentially even end up testifying before your state legislature or Congress on behalf of a bar group.

- **To advance your business development goals.** If your practice is supported by referrals by other lawyers, or if you practice in an area that often requires involvement by numerous lawyers—complex litigation, perhaps, or large corporate transactions—bar associations can create the opportunity for you to become known by your potential referral sources. You may also receive referrals from lawyers who have been conflicted out of a particular representation and have come to respect you through your work together in the association.

- **To have fun.** When you find a group that is a good fit for you, networking and conferences become a time to reconnect with friends as well as to accomplish something of professional benefit. You will be more likely to participate actively with a group of people you enjoy. As an added benefit, you may find that professional relationships progress over a period of years into rich personal friendships.

Industry Organization Involvement

If your goal is to meet potential clients through organizational involvement, you will probably experience greater benefits from becoming active in an industry or affinity organization than from bar association activity. Your potential clients likely congregate in some kind of group, and to meet those clients, you should travel in the same professional circles. Reasons to investigate joining an industry organization include:

- **Meeting large numbers of your potential clients and referral sources.** If you are a family lawyer, for example, you may find that most of your business comes via referral and that meetings of a local chapter of the Association of Marriage and Family Counselors are filled to the brim with potential referral sources.
- **Developing relationships with potential clients and referral sources in the absence of competitive lawyers.** More and more lawyers are discovering the benefit of getting involved in industry groups. Here you are likely to find opportunities to engage your potential clients and referral sources through committee work or other activities in which few

lawyers with directly competitive markets join. Many lawyers make the mistake of joining industry groups simply to get a credential, and they fail to become active. Their loss is your gain

Sometimes, however, you will find that your relevant industry group is swarming with other lawyers. If so, you may need to be creative and search for another organization or a committee that has not been overrun with lawyers.

- **Contributing to the legal knowledge of your target audience.** If you are active in an industry organization, you will almost certainly have opportunities to share a legal perspective on business issues. Whether you do so one–on–one or (preferably) through articles and presentations that extend your reach to a wider audience, you can share information that the other members will find useful. By doing so, you demonstrate your authority, which puts you in a strong position for business development purposes.

- **Learning about your ideal clients' perspective.** One enormous benefit of joining industry organizations is that you have an opportunity to learn about the concerns of your ideal clients. By noting the topics of articles and meetings, and through conversation with members, you will have your finger on the pulse of your ideal clients. You will then be able to respond to questions and concerns quickly, by sharing relevant information or by discussing how your services might meet any worries expressed. You will also gather information useful for targeting articles and presentations to your ideal clients, so you will never have to wonder what they need to know now.

- **Discovering issues that impact your clients as they arise.** When you join an industry organization, you will be privy to information about new developments that affect the industry and therefore affect your clients in that sector of business. You can take that knowledge back to your current clients to propose proactive measures to deal with the issues, demonstrating your attention to your clients' needs and perhaps creating opportunities for new business.

Examples of industry groups include the Biotechnology Industry Organization, the American Bankers Association, and the National Association of Industrial and Office Properties. You can locate these groups in at least two ways. The first and most beneficial is by asking current clients in the industry you would like to target. When you approach a client and tell him that you enjoy your work together, want to learn more about his field, and would like to join a relevant association that he recommends, you will get feedback about which groups are most attractive to that client and others like him. That approach will, moreover, demonstrate your interest in the client and in his business, and you may also realize additional benefits from demonstrating that interest.

When you find a group that is a good fit for you, networking and conferences become a time to reconnect with friends as well as to accomplish something of professional benefit.

If you seek to explore a business area in which you have not yet developed any work, you can do research on the Internet by typing in search phrases such as "pharmaceutical organizations," for example, or you might consult *The Directory of Associations,* a subscription–based online compendium of organizations with a list of over 600 industries.

Becoming Active in an Organization

Whether you decide to join a bar association or an industry–focused organization, you must become an active member to realize the full potential of that pursuit. Passive membership may be useful for your own educational purposes, because many organizations strive to deliver content to members through listservs, newsletters, journals, and programs delivered in person or via teleconference or webinar. Simply receiving information may help you to decide whether you want to become more involved with a particular group, but do not mistake simply being a member of a group or a committee for being active.

To become known and to develop robust credentials, you must attend meetings regularly and actively participate in some aspect of the group's activities. Moving into a leadership position is particularly helpful. As a leader, you further leverage your time (becoming known by many more people than you would in one–on–one encounters) and you will likely make some substantive contribution to the organization.

Fortunately, attaining a leadership position can be accomplished with relative ease in many organizations. First, identify a subgroup of the organization that you find interesting. Look through the sections, committees and subcommittees, or the list of projects that the group maintains. Your goal is to identify a small working group that will be a good fit for your skills, your interests, and your goals, in that order. You should focus on what you can contribute to the group, not what you might be able to get from it. By doing so, you bring value to the group.

Working groups almost always need help. Decide how much time you have available and what kind of assistance you would like to offer. Because you will be establishing a reputation for how you work, ensure that you have sufficient time to deliver fully on any commitment you make. Acquiring a reputation for being an unreliable volunteer can cause substantial damage, especially if you are working in an industry organization in which your potential clients mingle.

To become known and to develop robust credentials, you must attend meetings regularly and actively participate in some aspect of the group's activity.

You may be able to get a feel for current projects from the group's website. If not, or if you are aware of an issue that merits the group's attention, develop a short proposal for a project. What issue would you study? What work product would you create? Having spent some time as a passive member of the group will be helpful if you are creating a new proposal, because you will have a sense of how the group operates and whether a proposal to generate a report or a panel discussion (for example) might be more successful.

In the absence of that experience, you can probably access a great deal of information through the organization's website. Acquaint yourself with the group's activities over the past two or three years so you can ensure that you are proposing something new and that your proposal is in keeping with the group's operating style.

Contact the leader of a subgroup you would like to join and volunteer. For all but the most prestigious groups, a committee chair's favorite words to hear are probably, "I would like to help!" Discover how you can make a contribution. Look for something fairly short–term, so you are not boxed in and can prove yourself quickly. Do not, for instance, propose to rewrite model rules for the industry's operations as your first project. While such a project may be worthy and might net you substantial attention, such a large undertaking is not the best place to start. Volunteer for a discrete project and do a good job on it.

During and following the course of your project, and ideally before it begins, attend the business meetings of your selected group. Most associations meet on a regular basis, and those who attend business meetings tend to be the leaders and the active participants. If you want to become a leader, meet them. Learn more about the group's activity, which members are involved, what the group's history is, and how it operates.

Most associations meet on a regular basis, and those who attend tend to be the leaders and the active participants. If you want to become a leader, meet them.

Ask about the leadership track—how might you become a committee leader, a section leader, or an association leader? Making such an inquiry shows your interest in the group and your potential interest in joining the leadership. You will need to evaluate the group's culture before delving into that investigation, however: some groups have a *de facto* succession plan, and others seek new blood regularly. Contribute to the conversation and volunteer where appropriate. Show your interest and your ability.

Once you have taken on a few projects and performed well, you will start to advance. Especially if you do attend the group's business meetings and make strong contacts within the leadership, your work is likely to be noticed quickly.

Depending on the group, you can probably expect to become a subcommittee vice chair (or some equivalent title) within a couple of years, and sometimes much faster. Should you choose to advance in leadership, you will know much more about how to do so in your selected group; if not, you can probably continue at your current level of involvement and accrue additional benefits.

The Bottom Line for Reluctant Rainmakers

Organizational involvement offers the opportunity to learn and enhance your credentials. If undertaken strategically, it also puts you directly in front of ideal clients and referral sources, where you can parlay active involvement in the group into new business. Note that the key word here is active: if you choose to be a passive member of an organization, you will realize many fewer benefits. As with other rainmaker activities, set your strategy first and then tailor your organizational involvement to meet your objectives.

Chapter 10

Visiting Your Clients

One simple and too–often overlooked opportunity to deepen your professional relationship with a client is to offer an on–site visit. Particularly if your client is a business organization, visiting the headquarters, local office, or factory can demonstrate your interest in learning about your client and its business. While a visit to a client's home may be less appropriate depending on the type of representation and the relationship already developed, in some matters a home visit may be exactly the kind of value–added service that would distinguish you from competitors. For example, you might visit personal injury clients at home while they are recovering, or you could offer in–home estate planning for homebound clients. When preparing to suggest a site visit, you should consider several aspects of a visit, including the purpose, whether the visit is "on the clock," and what next steps might be appropriate.

Your visit will likely have one of three primary purposes, or perhaps a combination of them:

- **To facilitate the representation.** If, for example, you are representing a defendant in a process patent infringement case, you will likely find it far easier to understand the matter if you visit the manufacturing facility and see the relevant process in action. You might also need to conduct a site visit to interview potential witnesses, view an accident scene, or review a client's method of record–keeping. Similarly, if your family law client is homebound or if visiting your office is simply too difficult for some reason, meeting the client at his home or workplace may be helpful and much appreciated.
- **To develop the relationship.** Sometimes a visit is not necessary to an engagement, but you may sense that you could learn more about the client, his business, employees, and industry by meeting at his office. Site visits also offer an ideal opportunity to meet the business representatives in person and to have conversations about how they would like the engagement to operate: what mode of communication they prefer, how frequently they would like a status update, and so on. These visits are, therefore, especially valuable at the beginning of an engagement. They are also helpful at the end of an engagement to get a sense of the client's satisfaction with the outcome of the matter and the service you have provided. These are the conversations that might also provide a springboard to additional engagements.
- **Client education.** It may become apparent that an in–person meeting would be useful to help a client better understand the scope or impact of the matter

on which you have been retained. Alternatively, you may uncover new developments in the law or in the client's industry that call for proactive response. In either case, you might consider an on–site visit to educate your client and, if appropriate, to propose next steps. Educational visits may be as formal as a seminar for some of the client's employees or as casual as a conversation over a cup of coffee.

Each of these reasons for an on–site visit tends to dictate whether the meeting should be billable or provided as a client service. If the meeting is necessary for the engagement, it generally should be billable; if it is designed solely to develop the relationship or to educate the client about a matter outside the scope of the representation, it generally should not be billable. Consider what the client will expect and what would best serve the client when you decide whether to charge for a visit or to provide it off the clock. And whatever your decision, be clear with the client: an unbilled meeting might come as a pleasant surprise (because you would, of course, note the time on your invoice and mark it "no charge"), but a meeting unexpectedly billed could do irreparable harm to a client relationship.

> ***When suggesting a site visit, consider several aspects of the visit, including the purpose, whether the visit is "on the clock," and what next steps might be appropriate.***

Following your site visit, you should make notes

about what you learned. If the client gave you guidance regarding how the matter should run, be sure to share that information with any members of the client service team who were not present for the meeting. Next, determine what kind of follow–up contact would be helpful to your client. If the primary purpose of your visit was to educate your client on a new circumstance that could impact its business, perhaps you should send supporting information such as a copy of an article (preferably yours) discussing the new regulation or case and outlining what response would best protect the client. Alternatively, you might suggest a luncheon meeting with the client and a colleague who could contribute to a discussion about the new developments. At a minimum, be sure to send the client a note to show your appreciation for the time.

The Bottom Line for Reluctant Rainmakers

Site visits can be a simple way to bring additional value to a client and to develop a relationship of mutual trust and confidence. Determine whether such visits might be useful by asking your clients, if you are uncertain, or by offering to visit when you believe the circumstances are appropriate. Because such visits are unusual, you may set yourself apart from other lawyers with this approach. You may, as a result, receive repeat engagements and referrals from clients who are delighted with your service.

Chapter 11

Offering Seminars

Delivery to Clients

Providing seminars to clients offers a tremendous opportunity to showcase your expertise and to provide a valuable service to the client. This might be in response to a specific need you discover in the course of ordinary conversation with a client, or you could develop, over time, two or three general presentations that would be helpful to your clients. Whenever you deliver a well–received CLE presentation or write an article that garners positive feedback, consider whether it would be an appropriate topic for a client presentation. Seminars may be delivered on–site at the client's office, or (if appropriate for your area of practice) you might invite a selection of your clients to a presentation and reception in your office. In either case, remember that your goal is two–fold: first, to deliver useful content, and second, to build your relationship with the client.

Delivery to "Warm Contacts"

Offering an educational seminar to contacts with whom you have some relationship can be a powerful business development tool. Likewise, you may have referral sources through whom you could offer such a seminar to their clients or network. You will be speaking to audiences composed of people who know you either directly or through your contact who issued the invitation. Having already established at least one prong of the "know, like, and trust" factors, you have a better opportunity to develop the other two elements through your presentation and through interactions with the audience.

As is true of presentations delivered to strangers, most of the attendees either will not currently have legal needs or will already be represented by another lawyer and reasonably satisfied with that lawyer's service. Even so, you stand a better likelihood of attracting business when you present to a crowd of acquaintances than to a crowd of strangers.

Your goal is to offer useful information on a topic of interest to the audience, to establish your expertise in the matter, and to present yourself as a resource. Begin by identifying a topic for your seminar. The most successful topics are timely, either because of recent developments or because your audience will be considering the issues at hand when you offer the seminar. Examples of good topics include:

- **Wills and trusts for new parents**, who may not yet have any sort of estate planning and may be focusing for the first time on choosing a guardian for their child (or children) if both parents should die or be incapacitated.

- **Legal rights of same–sex couples**, which may be necessary in states that have not legalized gay marriage.
- **Electronically stored information and discovery**, a topic that was particularly relevant following the 2006 amendments to the Federal Rules of Civil Procedure and the new guidance on e–discovery.
- **Laboratory notebook maintenance,** a patent law primer for laboratory scientists, with a focus on what scientists must and must not do to record dates and other information that may become critical in patent prosecution or litigation.

The list of potential topics is limitless. When you select a topic, focus on a narrow scope that will be relevant and useful to the audience, regardless of whether they have current legal needs. For example, a topic that is procedurally specific (such as how to prepare to give a deposition) would be less beneficial, since most lawyers will prepare their own clients for deposition and since few people would be willing to attend such a seminar unless they expected to be deposed in the near future.

Choose a topic that falls within what you consider the heart of your practice: if most of your work is a traditional divorce practice and you are known for that work, offering a seminar on collaborative law would be less likely to generate substantial new business for you than a topic addressing the documentary issues a spouse should consider before filing for divorce. If, however, you are seeking to expand your collaborative law practice, providing a series of seminars describing the benefits of collaborative law could help you to broaden your practice in that direction.

The structure of your seminar should follow that of the oral presentations described in Chapter 6: tell stories that place the listener in a client's position and illustrate how you helped the client achieve her objectives. Be sure to close with an offer that will prompt the audience members to contact you. Perhaps you could produce a checklist relevant to the presentation, or you might invite audience members to subscribe to your newsletter that will provide ongoing information.

> ***Your goal is to offer useful information on a topic of interest to the audience, to establish your expertise in the matter, and to present yourself as a resource.***

As with any other presentation, your effort does not end with the seminar itself. Because you or a close contact of yours will have invited the attendees, it is generally appropriate to send each attendee a note following the seminar, expressing your appreciation for their presence and offering to provide further information. Determine too how you can repurpose your presentation. You might have it recorded and transcribed for easy editing into articles or blog posts, or you might consider offering it to other groups.

The Bottom Line for Reluctant Rainmakers

When you offer seminars to clients or to warm contacts, your audience will perceive you as the authority in the field who delivers valuable information. Reluctant rainmakers often enjoy content–centered modes of business development, and teaching a seminar fits perfectly within that preference. By designing follow–up contacts so you can remain in touch with your seminar audience, you can reinforce your expertise, perhaps while delivering additional useful information. These additional touches can further position you as a resource in the field, which (especially with ongoing follow–up over time) can lead to business.

Chapter 12

Networking

What occurs to you when you first see the word "networking"? For many reluctant rainmakers, networking conjures an image of a room packed with sweaty people wearing polyester suits and trying to foist their business cards on anyone unfortunate enough to be standing near them. Fortunately, that image has nothing at all to do with good networking. Good networking is simply the process through which relationships are started and developed. If you have a strongly negative reaction to the idea of networking, think back to your first days in law school.

You probably arrived at the new student orientation, perhaps knowing a few people but most likely not. You walked into a crowd of strangers with whom you had a common bond and some shared background, and you began the process of meeting your classmates. Although you may not have found an instant connection with anyone on the first day, you probably did develop enough interest in a few people to generate good conversation over lunch or coffee. Most likely, you sought out those same people over the next few days, while meeting new classmates as well, and over the course of three years, you developed close friendships with some students, warm acquaintance relationships with a larger number of students, and just enough familiarity to chat briefly or wave in passing to a still larger group. Over time, you got to know a sizeable number of your law school colleagues, learned whom you could trust (and whom not), and built solid relationships that began with a focus on your legal studies and in time developed into personal friendship as well. That experience represents good networking.

> ***You should network with people you have identified as being your ideal clients and referral sources.***

Networking is the process of building relationships and moving from strangers to acquaintances and (in some cases) deeper professional relationships. Successful networking comes down to three key questions: *who, how,* and *then what*. With whom should you network? How should you network with them? And once you have engaged in formal networking, then what? Learn to answer those questions well, and you will learn to succeed in networking.

With Whom Should You Network?

The first question you must answer is perhaps the most obvious. With whom should you network to maximize your chances of getting the results you desire? Your business development plan provides the short answer to this question. You should network with those whom you have identified as being your ideal clients and referral sources. A better question is: in what forums should you network to meet your ideal clients and referral sources? To answer that question, you need to think beyond the individual ideal clients and referral sources whom you would like to meet. Take the next step by identifying where those people—or the people who represent those organizations, if your ideal clients are corporations or other business organizations—congregate.

The first rule of networking is that, to be successful, you must fish in the right pond. Dave, a trademark lawyer who was a member of a rainmaker group I led, had identified his ideal clients as technology–based small businesses and start–up companies with less than $1 million in annual revenue. An extrovert, Dave had no problem meeting people and developing relationships that extended past business connections into warm professional friendships.

When he joined the rainmaker group, though, he announced that networking was not a viable strategy for him, because he had attended several organizations' meetings for over a year, had grown relationships, but had landed no new business as a result. I asked Dave which organizations he had joined, and the answer explained his lack of results. He had joined Habit for Humanity, the Jaycees, and the trademark committee of his state bar.

I asked Dave how many members of those organizations fit within his ideal client profile, and he replied that fewer than three people he had met at any of them did so. When I asked whether he could identify members who would be good referral sources for him, he at first said yes, but when pressed to name someone who had offered a referral, he was unable to do so. As I told Dave, there is nothing wrong with any of the organizations he had joined, and each could in theory be a good group for him. But none offered a heavy concentration of his target audience, and sifting through all of the people who did not meet his ideal client or referral source profile was taking far too much time and yielding poor results. Dave recognized that his organizational involvement was well–designed to raise his community and bar involvement and to add some credentials to his biographical sketch, but it was not the right fit for business development.

Dave returned to his business development plan and worked to identify which organizations would be composed of his ideal clients and others who would be in a position to refer those clients to him. He decided to focus on two organizations: a technology resource group that met regularly to deliver programs of interest to start–up and small technology companies, and an incubator group at a nearby university. By focusing on organizations that his ideal clients would attend, Dave was able to increase the number of potential clients he met, to develop relationships with those people, and to bring in business as a result, both directly from his contacts and through referrals they made to him.

Because community involvement was important to Dave, he continued to work with Habitat for Humanity and used his connections there to organize a home–building day for technology companies, so that even his community involvement put him in closer touch with his ideal client market. By making the shift from fishing in the wrong pond to fishing in the right pond, Dave was able to grow his client base by 150% over one year.

How can you identify the right organizations for your purposes? First, refresh your recollection of your ideal clients and referral sources, and then check the strategy you have devised for meeting those people. (Unless you completed your business development plan in the last month, take a few minutes to look at it again now even if you think you remember what it says. Lawyers will often spend time polishing a plan, only to set it aside when it is complete. Unless you review it regularly and view it as a living document, it will be of limited use to you.) Your plan should include a specific description of the people you want to meet; if not, review Chapter 3 and update your plan.

> ***Take a few minutes to look at your business development plan. Unless you review it regularly and view it as a living document, it will be of limited use to you.***

Do a bit of research (or better yet, delegate that research) to find the groups that those people might attend. Dave, for example, conducted an online search for "technology organization" in his city and discovered not just the groups with which he became involved, but also that a group of technology companies had established an organization for their general counsels. Dave was later able to speak at one of those meetings as well.

If your business development plan does not provide clear guidance as to where you should network to find your ideal clients and referral sources, answer the following questions to help specify the best groups for you to attend.

- What are the common features of my ideal clients and referral sources?

- What are their common interests?
- What business circumstances concern them?
- What kind of educational opportunities might they seek?
- What are their professions likely to be?
- Will they likely attend national or local meetings?

These questions will help you focus on where you might be able to find the kind of people with whom you should be networking. You might also consider working backward based on substantive area of practice. For example, if you are an estate planner, think about where large numbers of people who might hire estate planners or refer clients to estate planners would congregate.

As you identify organizations that may be fertile for your networking, be sure each one is likely to feature a large number of people within your target audience. Networking, at least in its most basic form, is a numbers game. You are likely to meet a large number of people who have no current need for your legal services or whose needs are being met by another lawyer with whom they are satisfied. As a result, you must reach a sufficient number of people to create the likelihood that a few people may have current, unmet legal needs.

Consider too whether your focus is on meeting potential clients or referral sources, because different groups may be present in different organizations. If your ideal clients are high net–worth individuals going through a divorce, you may choose to network with financial planners who would be in a position to make referrals to you. Why? First, you are more likely to find a group of financial planners than a group comprised of wealthy people who are divorcing and second, because most people are unwilling to talk about their personal situation to near–strangers, you may find it difficult to start substantive conversations with your ideal clients in an ordinary networking setting.

How Should You Network with Them?

Once you have identified a suitable group, you must develop a plan and a strategy for the networking itself. Most lawyers who are not successful in building business through networking focus on talking about themselves and their services rather than listening to their conversation partners. In contrast, successful networkers know that there are three key phases of a good networking conversation: (1) the approach and initiation of conversation, (2) learning about your conversation partner, and (3) sharing what you do and how you might help the person with whom you are talking. Phase 2 should be the focus of a good networking conversation.

The approach and initiation can be quite simple, though some lawyers find it extremely off–putting to walk into a room of strangers and begin a conversation. One easy way to handle this is to arrive early, before the room fills. Alternatively, consider attending an event with a colleague, but do not allow yourself to get lulled into conversation with that colleague. You can take turns introducing each other and highlighting experience or skill (pay careful attention to the subsequent discussion in this section so you do so proficiently), you can part ways to maximize the number of attendees you meet as a team, an look to each other for help in getting out of g conversations.

..ample, Janice, a coaching client whose practice focused on representing midsize corporations in employment matters, preferred to go to meetings attended by human resources personnel with Peter, a colleague with a similar practice. Janice and Peter would enter the room together and part ways quickly. Each would start a conversation with someone, and when Peter's conversation had run its course, he would join Janice's conversation and she would introduce him in the context of the conversation. (And if Janice's conversation ended first, the roles would reverse.) After a few minutes, Janice would excuse herself from the conversation, leaving Peter to continue; she would move on to meet someone else, and the cycle would continue. After the event, Janice and Peter would compare notes on the people whom they had met, decide with whom to follow up and how, and make a preliminary evaluation of the meeting's usefulness.

The three key phases of a good networking conversation are: (1) the approach and initiation of conversation, (2) learning about your conversation partner, and (3) sharing what you do and how you might help.

Another approach for starting a conversation is to look for someone standing alone, preferably someone who looks even less comfortable than you feel. If you spot someone who is standing on the fringe of the group, your opening gambit becomes almost irrelevant because the person you approach likely will be delighted to join a conversation. To prepare conversational openers, be sure to do a quick scan of the news before you leave for the event, and watch for any quirky or offbeat stories. Any news will work in a pinch, of course, but you are much more likely to launch a conversation well with something unexpected than by commenting on the weather.

The easiest conversational initiation of all is also perhaps the most effective. Ask how the person came to be at this event. Broad, open–ended questions tend to work best. "What brings you to this meeting today/tonight?" "How active are you with this group?" "What is your interest in [a topic relevant to the organization or meeting]?" Questions such as these will usually prompt a conversation in which the speaker discloses something about himself, which gives you some information and serves as the perfect segue into asking questions about your partner and learning more about him.

Consider what you need to know to help determine whether someone you meet is a likely candidate for your services or to refer you to others. Some lawyers are able to define their ideal clients with such precision that a few questions will rule someone in or out of that group. If, for example, your ideal client is a start–up biotechnology company with no in–house legal counsel and a need for angel investors, you will be able to ask a few questions and determine whether the person with whom you are speaking is working in such a company.

If your ideal client description is less tightly defined, perhaps if your practice is limited to plaintiff's personal injury work, you may be unable to qualify the person with whom you are talking simply based on what you learn from her. Remember, though, that even if the person with whom you are speaking does not fall within your ideal client description, she may know others who do.

As you engage in conversation designed to learn more about the person with whom you are talking, consider asking questions like these:

- How is business these days?
- What changes have you noticed as a result of the economy?
- What changes do you see on the horizon for your business?
- Who are you hoping to meet at this event?
- Who is your ideal client?
- What is your top concern these days?

A common question is when to end a conversation if you discover that your conversation partner is not within your target client or referral group, or if you find that he is already represented by a lawyer and is happy with the service he is receiving. The classic lawyer's answer is appropriate here: it depends. On the one hand, if you have a good rapport with someone and that person is well–connected, you may benefit from a relationship even though it is unlikely to yield business in the short term. If, however, you are attending an event that is populated by people who match your ideal client or referral profile, you would probably be better advised to seek out those people and to have shorter conversations with others who are not a match. The desired outcome from networking is relationship generation, and you do not want to be the person who meets, evaluates, and then discards those who may not be useful for you. At the same time, you do need to invest your time primarily in those with whom you are more likely to have some professional connection.

The common feature of these questions is the focus on your conversation partner, the gentle probing for ways in which you might offer assistance, and inquiries designed to learn more about her. When you are asking questions, allow your natural curiosity (bounded by good etiquette) to guide you. Your goal, whether or not the person with whom you are talking matches your ideal client or referral description, is to learn about that person and her needs.

Do not hesitate to ask more personal questions as well. The process in which you and your conversational partner may begin to know, like, and trust each other often calls for personal revelation. You might start with social chit–chat, perhaps by commenting on the traffic that you had to battle to reach the event, which may lead into a conversation about the areas of town in which you and your networking companion live and work, and then into a discussion about a book that one of you has been listening to on CD during your daily commute, and then onward to other topics. If you feel uncomfortable making small talk, review the books recommended in the Rainmaker's Resource List at http://www.TheReluctantRainmaker.com.

Talking About Yourself

Once you have engaged in enough conversation to know something about the person with whom you are talking, conversation will usually shift naturally to you. At this point, resist the urge to launch immediately into your elevator speech. Pause instead to consider whether there is anything you can offer to help your companion. Perhaps you know someone who matches this person's ideal client profile, someone who is an expert in your contact's area of concern, or someone who would otherwise be a good connection. Or maybe you are aware of an article (perhaps one that you wrote) or a resource that would be helpful. This is the time to make that offer. Ask for the person's business card and make a note of the introduction you would like to make or the resource you would like to share, and then (and only then) begin to talk about yourself.

It is a good idea to have an "elevator speech" prepared. These self–introductions are called elevator speeches because they should last no more than 30 seconds, the amount of time you might spend between floors in an elevator. They should be designed to give key information about yourself and your practice, ideally in an interesting way. Most lawyers simply offer their area of practice, with a statement such as, "I'm a litigator" or "I do estate planning." While there is nothing wrong with such a factual statement, it is unlikely to grab anyone's attention. Instead, you may choose one of the following approaches to craft a more appealing elevator speech:

- **The benefits–focused description.** The typical elevator speech follows a template, such as "I help ______ to ______ by _______ so that they can ______." An example: "I help small businesses to maximize their net profits through careful tax planning so they can grow quickly and pass on more of the company's hard–earned profit to its owners." Or, "I help pharmaceutical companies with annual revenue in the range of $2 million to get the cash they need by negotiating funding deals so that they can conduct clinical trials of drugs in development." These elevator speeches may lack panache, but they offer results–oriented information that will allow your conversational partner to understand quickly what you do.

- **The practice– and client–centric description.** You could focus on the type of law you practice and the clients you represent. "I represent people who have suffered a traumatic brain injury in litigation against whoever caused the injury."
- **The USP introduction.** As discussed in Chapter 3, you should know how to describe your Unique Selling Proposition or USP. You can use that USP to craft an introduction, such as, "I prepare technology transfer agreements that draw on my background in tax law, so my clients never have to wonder whether they've missed important tax implications."
- **The provocative statement.** You might create an unusual way of describing what you do, one which will prompt your listener to respond, "Really? How do you do that?" If you can provoke such a response, your elevator speech has done its job, because the listener will surely pay close attention to what you say next. For example, if you practice tax law, you might say, "I work with small businesses to help them beat Uncle Sam—legally!" If you try a provocative introduction, you must be prepared to deliver it with a sense of humor and timing, and you should have another form of elevator speech that you can use as a back–up if your statement falls flat.

- **The "you know how" introduction.** Using this approach, you cast the problem that you solve for clients in a common, easily–understandable "you know how" framework: "You know how often a couple who's no longer happy together decide to divorce and the situation turns into an absolute disaster, with each spouse blaming the other and trying to get any possible advantage, with the result that everyone comes out a loser in the end? Well, I work with divorcing spouses *before* all of that begins, using an approach called collaborative law. I represent one spouse and another collaborative lawyer represents the other spouse, and we sit down together to find a way to end the marriage without starting World War III."

Regardless of the format you use to prepare your elevator speech, it must be short, descriptive, conversational, attention–grabbing, and benefits–focused. You may want to develop more than one elevator speech so you can tailor your introduction to your audience. If you are speaking to another lawyer, for instance, the use of legal terms of art will be expected and welcome, assuming the terms you use are reasonably comprehensible and not jargon used in a field in which the other lawyer does not practice. If you are speaking to a non–lawyer about your consumer law practice, the language you use should paint a clear image of your practice without using any jargon.

Be sure to practice your elevator speech so that it is well–crafted, but avoid sounding canned. No matter how good your introduction is, if it sounds as if you could roll it off in your sleep, it is unlikely to attract positive feedback and continued conversation. In fact, you might try using bullet points to outline your speech rather than writing and memorizing it in its entirety.

> ***Regardless of the format you use to prepare your elevator speech, it must be short, descriptive, conversational, attention–grabbing, and benefits–focused.***

Your elevator speech must serve two objectives. First, it must educate the listener about your work. Second, and more importantly, it must engage the listener and provide a reason and a path to continue the conversation. With luck, you consider your area of practice and your work to be at least mildly interesting, and you should be able to develop an elevator speech that conveys your enthusiasm.

Lest you imagine that interesting introductions are reserved for those who take death penalty cases or represent celebrities, consider the introduction that one of my coaching clients loved to give: "I'm Peter Eppler, and I hold the city responsible when its construction crews goof up and make a curb a half–inch too high, causing our good citizens to trip and hurt themselves." Peter, a plaintiffs' lawyer, used this introduction to catch attention and to distinguish himself from other personal injury lawyers.

Almost without exception, the person with whom he was talking would be startled by his introduction and ask something about how a half–inch could possibly make such a difference. Peter would tell the story of a client who was badly injured after catching her heel on such a curb, and he would share his astonishment that a well–respected expert testified that even a half–inch variation in curb height could cause accidents.

He would then go on to explain that he learned the importance of tiny details through that case, and that he always thought of that client when facing an argument that a defendant should not be held liable for some minor act or omission. Deeply enthralling? No, but interesting enough to continue the conversation and memorable enough to ensure that no one who heard his story would forget Peter's area of practice.

If you are able to engage someone in conversation enough to learn what she does, to share what you do, and to find a connection on a professional or personal basis, your networking is complete—for the moment.

Then What? The Art of the Follow–up

The first thing you must know about following up with the people you meet while networking is that you absolutely have to do it. If you do not plan to follow up on a networking conversation, you need not bother trying to grow your network. It will not work. One of the mistakes I see lawyers making far too often in networking is thinking that the networking itself will yield the results. In fact, networking is only the beginning of a relationship. Without follow–up, no relationship will develop, and without a relationship and continued contact, it is unlikely that you will ever see any business results from your networking activity.

Cathy, an IP litigator in a large firm who was trying to grow her network for both business development and job search purposes, hired me to help her develop and then implement a career strategy. Before we started working together, I asked her what she was doing to grow her network. She was taking part in some good activities, including attending her area's Women in Technology meetings, Licensing Executive Society committee meetings, and her state bar association's IP Section meetings. Cathy had joined these groups in hopes of landing new business and learning about potential lateral moves that she might want to investigate.

When I asked how effective the networking was for those purposes, Cathy was uncertain. She was unable to name even one person who had provided an opportunity to her or to whom she had made recommendations of any sort. I asked Cathy what kinds of ongoing relationships she had, perhaps regular lunch meetings or a group of people she would sit with during each meeting, but she told me that she had avoided repeat contact along those lines so that she could meet a lot of people and not get locked into a group.

Finally, I asked whom from these groups she would call if she needed to make a referral to a lawyer or to someone else who works with technology companies in some capacity. Cathy could not name anyone and told me that she did not have a clear enough idea of what any of her contacts did to feel comfortable making such a referral. The diagnosis was simple: even though Cathy was meeting lots of people, she had not created relationships that would yield the information and results she was seeking.

Research indicates that most people need to see at least seven to nine "impressions" before they become aware of who you are and what you do. An impression is any kind of contact, such as chatting with you at a meeting, having a conversation over coffee or lunch, seeing your name in the local business journal, getting an e-mail from you, or seeing your profile pop up in social media. Following up with the people you meet is simply the process of creating those impressions. Because a single contact is so unlikely to result in any meaningful relationship, if you neglect the follow–up and fail to create the opportunities for repeated contact, networking is a poor investment of time, if not a complete waste.

Once you accept that you must follow up with the people whom you meet, you must decide how to execute a follow–up strategy. With whom do you follow up—everyone? When and how often? And most troubling for a lot of lawyers—how? Let's take those questions one by one.

Maintain Prioritized Contact Lists

Ideally, you would follow up with every person you meet, but the amount of time that would be required for that level of commitment is not feasible for most lawyers. Instead, divide your contacts into three lists: the A list, B list, and C list. As you might guess, the A list is composed of the people who are most likely to yield the results you seek, and it should be your smallest list. For business development purposes, the A list could include selected former clients who are likely to have additional legal needs that you might meet, people who have referred business to you more than once, and ideal clients with whom you have some connection. Your B list might include your other former clients, everyone who has referred business to you in the past, and selected "warm" contacts who may bring you business at some point in the future. Your C list includes essentially everyone else with whom you would like to maintain contact, and it will be the largest of your three contact lists.

List category	*Who is included*	*How often to contact*
A	Former clients who may have additional legal needs you could meet; repeat referral sources; ideal clients with whom you already have a connection	Every 4-6 weeks
B	All other former clients; all other referral sources; selected "warm" contacts	Quarterly
C	All those with whom you would like to maintain contact and who are not included on the A or B lists	Once or twice annually

The lists determine how often you make contact with each person on them. The A list is the group you will contact most often, generally in the range of every four to six weeks. The B list is the intermediate group, to be contacted quarterly, and the C list group will receive contact once or twice a year. By dividing your contacts into priority levels, you ensure that you keep in touch and stay top–of–mind with those whom you expect to be most likely to have legal needs you may meet. You also ensure that you continue relationships with others who are perhaps less immediately likely to yield business. These repeated contacts (whether monthly or annually) will keep relationships fresh and will allow you to use your follow–up time wisely.

Note that people may move from one list to another over time—sometimes in just an instant. A client who had just started using the A/B/C list approach told me that he had bumped into a former colleague, someone who was on his C list and had held the "occasional contact" status for many years. That former colleague vaulted to an A list position when she referred three litigation matters to my client following their conversation and remarked that she was delighted to have someone to whom she could refer good cases that she could not handle herself. My client speculated that, had he not made contact with her when he did, those referrals would likely have gone to another lawyer who was more immediately on his former colleague's radar screen. My client now receives referrals from his former colleague regularly, and he considers frequent contact with her to be a high value as well as a pleasure.

Newer lawyers might have a larger A list that will, over time, start distributing itself into the three lists. Most likely, a larger number of law school classmates will qualify as an A list member one year following graduation than will do so 10 years later. By the same token, many if not most of the people you meet will start out on your C list; some will move up the chain over time and many will not. To make sure that your contacts are included on the appropriate list, you will need to evaluate those lists on an ongoing basis. List assignment is not permanent.

Set Your Follow–up Strategy

Most lawyers' follow–up strategy is limited to sending an e-mail or a note after meeting a new contact and later inviting that contact to coffee or lunch. Successful follow–

up requires a repertoire of ways to keep in touch with your contacts, however. Because most people need to be exposed to you seven to nine times before you hold a spot in their consciousness, you must have a number of options at your fingertips to establish fresh, non–repetitive contact. The following examples are good choices:

- **Use Google Alerts** to receive information about your contacts or their businesses or industries via e-mail. Google Alerts allow you to set search terms and parameters so that relevant information is delivered directly to you by e-mail. You then use the information from the Alert for a follow–up contact. For instance, if you learn that one of your acquaintances just published a new article in a bar journal, you might read the article quickly and then send a note of congratulations.
- **Share information about legal changes.** If you become aware of a change in law or regulation that may affect a contact, you might offer to share the information accompanied by an analysis of the changes.
- **Invite your contact to a seminar.** If you plan to attend a seminar that a contact may find interesting, invite that person to join you. Be selective, however: think twice before inviting a contact to a meeting to listen to another lawyer in your area of practice.
- **Host an open house.** Your firm or office might host a seasonal open house designed to bring clients and contacts into your office.
- **Introduce a new colleague.** If a new lawyer joins

your firm and has substantial expertise in an area of interest to one of your contacts, consider inviting the two of them to lunch so that you can introduce them.

- **Send birthday cards.**
- **Send holiday cards.** You need not limit yourself to the standard holidays. Depending on your practice and your personality, you might consider recognizing off–beat holidays, such as National Napping Day, Panic Day, or the birthday of the explorer Amerigo Vespucci. Visit http://www.holidays.net/dailys.htm to find a list of daily holidays. This tactic will not fit every lawyer or every practice, to be sure, but if it is appropriate for your practice, you can make a strong impression since your contact will not be deluged by holiday cards on "fun" holidays.
- **Make introductions to other contacts.** If you discover that one of your contacts is looking for an accountant and you know a good accountant and make that introduction, you will put yourself in the position of a connector, someone who knows a variety of other people in the community and whose status is elevated accordingly. Be sure to vet your contacts before making introductions, though, because your reputation is at stake when you recommend people in your network to one another.
- **Make recommendations.** If you visit a terrific new Italian restaurant and know that one of your A list contacts loves Italian food, drop her an e-mail, or give her a quick call to recommend it. When you make a personal suggestion, you demonstrate that

you pay enough attention to your contacts to enable you to make good recommendations to them. You also show that you know what is new and interesting in your community.

- **Follow up on a recommendation a contact made to you.** This is the flip side of the previous suggestion. If someone recommends a restaurant or book or movie to you, let that person know that you followed his recommendation and that you enjoyed the experience. Assuming that you did benefit from the suggestion, circling back to express your appreciation is a nice follow-through and a good way to add another "impression."

- **Send a relevant book or magazine.** If you find a book or magazine to be especially meaningful or helpful for you and you think it would be useful for one of your contacts, send it to that person. Doing so is relatively inexpensive (and thus unlikely to be inappropriate) and demonstrates that the contact is sufficiently important to prompt you to go to the effort of acquiring and then sending a copy.

- **Send a helpful article or resource**, especially if you are the author. Perhaps in conversation with a contact you discovered that she is considering moving from a PC to a Mac and you later happen across an article comparing the two. Forward it on to your contact. This is even more effective if your contact has a legal quandary addressed by an article that you wrote, but non-legal resources are also effective to help you to build a relationship.

- **Send written materials about your practice.** If

your contact requests written materials about you, your firm, or your practice, take the opportunity for follow–up contact. Some lawyers carry marketing materials with them to a meeting. Sending them after the fact tends to be more effective because you have a built–in reason to reconnect and because sending them following your conversation will allow you to select the most useful materials, whereas you would have to make a guess about what would be helpful if you bring them with you to the meeting.

You might also consider requesting feedback from your contact about your materials. For example, a client who works with technology companies recently generated a marketing page that included a section titled, "Call me if…" and then listed several fact patterns that signal a situation within his practice. He asked a contact to review it and tell him whether the language connected. He received some good comments that helped him to sharpen the piece while educating his contact on his practice. Note that this approach succeeds only if the request for feedback is genuine. It will backfire if your contact catches even a whiff of insincerity in seeking an opinion.

- **Issue an invitation to lunch.** The lunch invitation is probably the most classic form of business follow–up. It is also among the most time–intensive. Before you invite a contact to lunch, know your objectives for the conversation.
- **Interact on social media.** Almost without exception, it is appropriate to send a LinkedIn

> request after you meet a new contact. If both you and your new contact are active users of social media, you may have opportunities to engage your new connection, which will help you to develop a relationship. Although LinkedIn is the *de facto* professional social media platform, you might consider interacting with contacts on other platforms as well, as discussed *infra* in Chapter 14.

The best follow–up methods are personal to your contact, simple to accomplish, and inexpensive. Select a few follow–up methods that suit you best and find ways to integrate them into your practice. Doing so forms the basis of a system to avoid having contacts slip away without your notice. Phase one of your system should ensure that every new contact receives a note or an e-mail from you. You will, of course, need to write the note, but decide that you will do so for each contact that merits continued communication. Add those people to your contact list in the appropriate category, and include a tickler to be sure that you follow up on the schedule you decide to implement.

Keeping your A list by your computer will facilitate regular contacts with the members of that list because you will have them on your mind and be more likely to notice when you read something that would interest one of them. Keep records of when you make contact and how. Request that your assistant track your activities and inform you when contact is due again (or you can create an automatic reminder using a tickler system) so you do not slip on the schedule.

So You Networked and Followed Up... What Now?

Once you have started networking in the appropriate organizations and following up with your new contacts, your thoughts should shift to how to measure your results and what steps to take next. Most relationships take some time to develop and to result in a referral, however, and you will probably find it discouraging to measure your results only in terms of business actually generated. Face–to–face meetings are the most effective for developing relationships and uncovering opportunities, and you should consider getting to such a meeting to be the primary objective for your contacts.

Once you get there, however, it is important to have a goal in mind so that you do not fall prey to the "random acts of lunch" problem in which you spend a great deal of time meeting with contacts but have no results to show. Being able to articulate a reason for requesting a meeting will also improve the probability that your contact will agree to join you.

> ***Face–to–face meetings are the most effective for developing relationships and uncovering opportunities.***

For example, if you are interested in sharing information on new regulations that promise to impact your contact's industry, making that purpose clear when you issue your invitation will likely entice your contact to accept, while she might be too busy to accept an invitation to lunch for nothing more than casual conversation.

During the meeting, after a few minutes of small talk

designed to make a connection, restate the objective for your meeting and be prepared to ask thoughtful questions. Even if you are sharing rather than seeking information, you will learn more and be better prepared to meet any legal needs you may uncover if you are able to get your contact's insight and feedback about the issues that interest her.

Through the process of developing relationships, you will have come to know enough about your contacts' businesses and about how they operate professionally to have some sense of whether you are likely to be able to generate business through them in the foreseeable future. Pause periodically to evaluate your success in networking. You may find that some activities or contacts that showed great promise initially have fizzled out, and you may find substantial potential in activities or contacts that you did not expect to bear fruit.

Remember that most of the contacts whom you meet will not have immediate legal needs or will be happily working with other lawyers, and remember that being of service will showcase your experience and expertise and will make others more likely to be interested in meeting with you, which in turn will provide you better odds of identifying opportunities.

The Bottom Line for Reluctant Rainmakers

Far from being shady opportunities to press the flesh and seek business in an exploitive, desperate manner, networking is the process of building relationships. Be certain that you strategically select the meetings you attend, so you meet people who may become or may introduce you to new clients. Remember to make it your goal to learn about your conversation partner before you begin to talk about yourself, and seek to offer something useful to each person whom you meet. Lay your plans to follow up on your networking meetings. If you fail to follow up on an initial meeting (or to continue following up at appropriate intervals), the time you spent making the contact is absolutely wasted. Finally, evaluate your networking success periodically so you can determine whether your current activities are meeting with enough success to justify continuing them.

Chapter 13

Newsletters and Legal Updates

Newsletters and legal updates offer a way to stay in contact easily with a large number of people. Legal updates are short, single–focused mailings that highlight a new case or other recent development relevant to your clients' interests and may be considered a subset of a newsletter, which is published on a regular schedule, typically with several articles or columns per issue. To simplify matters, this discussion will refer primarily to newsletters; unless otherwise noted, all comments apply equally to legal updates.

Because newsletters focus on substantive information, your outreach will be valuable to its recipients and therefore welcome. Better yet, if your topics are timely and if you include an appropriate call to action, you may even receive requests for assistance on matters related to your writing. You can also repurpose presentations and articles you have written for publication elsewhere into newsletter content, and, conversely, you can review your newsletters for ideas to use for future writing and speaking opportunities. Inject some personal commentary or information into a newsletter, and you will continue to build a relationship with your readers while leveraging your time by communicating one–to–many.

Newsletters may be sent electronically or by mail. E-mail newsletters have a substantial cost advantage and tend to be easier to create, but they are easier for would–be readers to overlook or put aside for later reading, with the common result that they are never read. Hard copy newsletters are a tangible representation of your firm, are easy to pass around to others, and (if retained) can bring you to top–of–mind each time the recipient happens across your newsletter, but they are significantly more expensive to prepare and send.

Focus on practical articles that include checklists, "to do" or "not to do" lists, and resources.

Your first decision, then, is what kind of newsletter you should use, or whether you should send both types. If you elect to use an electronic newsletter, you must invest in a delivery system that is tailored for this purpose. Do not use your own e-mail system. Using your own e-mail system to send hundreds or thousands of newsletters to subscribers almost guarantees that many of them will not be received and even that your domain may be blacklisted, which will prevent any of your e-mails from reaching their recipients. Examples of commercial delivery systems include Constant Contact, Aweber, and InfusionSoft. These systems are designed to send mass e-mails to an audience of subscribers. They include safeguards to prevent spammers from using the system and penalties for those reported by recipients to be spammers, so their delivery rates remain high.

Finally, decide to whom you will send your

newsletter. If you use electronic delivery, you must comply with the CAN–SPAM Act, and all of the above–identified delivery services do so. To avoid legal problems or being labeled an intrusive pest, be sure that you have permission to send your newsletter. Include a statement in client engagement letters that you publish a quarterly/monthly/weekly newsletter and will send it to the client unless she specifically requests not to receive it. You may send a sample issue to your contact list and invite them to be included on a future list, but it is bad form (and potentially legally problematic) to include your entire contact list on your newsletter distribution list without explicit permission.

The CAN–SPAM Act requires, and good etiquette demands, that you have permission to include someone on your subscription list. All delivery systems require that you have such permission, and all will terminate your account if too many recipients mark your e-mail as spam.

Having decided on the format, delivery system, and addressees for your newsletter, you must next consider the following:

- **Name.** Your newsletter must have a title. It need not be catchy, and you need not spend money developing a graphics-rich banner. Simple text is sufficient, and you can use a title as generic as "Smith & Jones Newsletter." Let your practice be your guide here: you might want to find a memorable title if your newsletter will go primarily to consumers, but you could use a more academic title if the bulk of your subscribers are general counsel. (Do not allow that distinction to justify a dull newsletter, however; general counsels want interesting reading material as much as anyone else.)

- **Content.** You can write or otherwise produce your own content, or you can contract with a service to provide information that will interest your subscribers. The best newsletters offer original content, whether written by you or drafted by someone else and edited to match your voice and perspective. Consider the range of topics you might include, as well as a varied format. Focus on practical articles that include checklists, "to do" or "not to do" lists, and resources. Add photographs or other graphics to make your newsletter more readable and eye–catching. Give thought to what kinds of non–law content might make your newsletter even more interesting to readers (and induce them to pass your newsletter on to others), and include some personal information about yourself or your staff if appropriate for your clientele.

- **Frequency of publication.** As a general rule, an e-mail newsletter should be circulated more frequently than a hardcopy newsletter. Although current research suggests that weekly e-mail newsletters are most effective, you might launch your newsletter on a monthly schedule and decide based on feedback whether to publish more frequently. Quarterly publication of hardcopy newsletters is probably sufficient, though monthly is preferable if not cost prohibitive.

You must remember, especially with respect to e-mail newsletters, that not every recipient will read every newsletter. The frequency of publication helps to increase the number of readers overall because those who skip an issue (and have not become disinterested) will be more likely to read the next issue if it comes relatively soon. If months pass before the next issue arrives, readers' enthusiasm for the newsletter may dim.

In contrast to newsletters, you should publish legal updates as often as circumstances require, which may mean sending two in a single week and then none for a few months. Because of legal updates' inconsistent publication, they are most effectively used as a supplement to monthly or quarterly newsletters when news would be stale by the time the next newsletter is published.

- **Length of newsletter.** The more frequently you publish your newsletter, the shorter it should be. Instead of including two articles, a case study, and a personal interest section in each newsletter, break up your content into shorter issues. Doing so will make your newsletter easier to read quickly, which decreases the risk of readers setting it aside intending to read it later, and instead discarding it the next time they come across it. You will also find it easier to fill a shorter newsletter, and you will be less tempted to abandon it if time gets short.
- **Call to action.** Every newsletter should include an appropriate request for readers to act. Consider your local ethics rules in creating this section, and be sure your invitation coincides with the tone your clients will expect. As with the call to action you would include in an externally published article or

a speech, your goal is to issue an invitation that will prompt those so inclined to contact you directly. Without such an invitation, readers may take your newsletter for informational purposes only, not realizing that you stand ready to assist if needed.

- **Repurpose your newsletter content.** You should include all newsletter articles on your website as a way to assist with organic search engine traffic and to provide a resource library for those who may be considering hiring you. Having such a library shows that you actively reach out and provide additional value to your clients and gives potential clients an additional method by which to evaluate you. One effective way to organize articles is to include a link on the front page of your website to the most recent newsletter copy and to the archives, with a list of all previously published articles (perhaps indexed by topic) on another page of your site. You can also repurpose your newsletter content by using a blog.

The Rainmaker Resource List (http://www.TheReluctantRainmaker.com) provides additional information and resources to help you build an effective newsletter that your clients and contacts will appreciate.

The Bottom Line for Reluctant Rainmakers

Using newsletters and legal alerts allows you to make regular contact with your network and to deliver information and analysis that will be helpful. By doing so, you present yourself as someone who is in touch with the needs of those who are interested in your area of practice and as an expert in addressing those needs. Finally, if you use a conversational tone and provide some news about yourself and your staff, you can leverage your time and build relationships with your readers so they may be comfortable discussing their legal needs with you when such needs arise. Regular delivery of beneficial information creates a "drip" approach that will keep you top-of-mind with your contacts without running the risk of seeming pushy.

Chapter 14

Social Media

Social media allows users to generate and share content and to interact using an Internet–based platform. Blogs are a form of social media, because bloggers author posts, share posts written by others, and generally welcome comments, albeit often with some oversight and moderation. Well–known social media applications include LinkedIn, Facebook, Google+, and Twitter. These platforms are considered to be social networking services, because users create an online community in which they can develop relationships online with people with whom they connect. In this way, online networking replicates in–person networking, creating the potential for people to meet, communicate with, and come to know, like, and trust one another without ever meeting in person or even speaking by voice.

Social media is a large and complex topic, and this chapter is designed to provide an overview of the ways in which lawyers might explore and benefit from social media. Numerous opportunities exist to engage in social media, and for reasons of economy, this chapter will offer only the tip of the iceberg, addressing first general audience social media (such as LinkedIn, Twitter, Google+, and Facebook) and then turning to platforms designed specifically for lawyers (such as JD Supra, Lawlink, LegallyMinded, and Legal Trends).

General Social Media

As with any form of networking, you must identify the kinds of people you would like to meet before you get started. A high percentage of social networkers rely on general purpose systems such as LinkedIn, Facebook, Google+, and Twitter. Each of these services attracts a diverse crowd of people. (Although many other networks exist, these four are the primary networks accepted for professional use.) Because of their popularity, content posted to LinkedIn, Facebook, and Twitter tends to be included in search engine results quickly. Google+ offers unparalleled benefits for search engine visibility, and users' social media profiles are often included among the top few Google search results for their names.

LinkedIn

LinkedIn is the most professionally oriented of the three networks: executives of all of the Fortune 500 companies use LinkedIn. As of late 2013, LinkedIn featured over 259 million mostly professional users spread across 200 countries; the average user is 44 years old with an average household income of $86,000. LinkedIn users construct a profile that includes their full educational and work history and request connections with people they actually know, locating them by search by contacts' name or through the use of an automated e-mail contact list tool. Unlike many social networking sites that encourage users to request a connection with anyone who might interest them, LinkedIn recommends establishing connections with people you already know. To discourage random connections requests, users have the option to click "I don't know this person" in response to a connection request and by doing so penalize the offending requester.

> ***If LinkedIn were an in-person gathering, it would be a networking breakfast.***

Selective invitations to connect are thus critical, and by bringing your offline network online via LinkedIn, you create the opportunity to discover interconnections. For example, you could learn that the banker you meet for a networking breakfast every week is connected to the CEO of the healthcare company you have identified as an ideal client. You might find that connection in the offline world, but with more steps in between your immediate contact and your target—the banker who knows the accountant who knows the employee benefits specialist who knows the healthcare company's CEO, for example—LinkedIn represents by far your best opportunity to network your way to the people you would like to meet. The system displays only first– and second–degree connections (remember the consanguinity charts from your law school trusts and estate class?), but by broadening your connections, you increase the chance of working your way through to the people you hope to meet.

Communications are somewhat limited on LinkedIn. You can exchange messages (similar to e-mail) with another user, you can participate in discussions held in groups (which may be open to all or available only for those approved by the group's administrator, and you can share an update.

You may also request and write recommendations for other LinkedIn users with whom you have worked in some capacity. The recommendations tend to be meaningful (in other words, more than "Joe is a great lawyer") and are considered to be an important part of the LinkedIn system because they add credibility to your profile and offer information that others will consider when connecting with you. In contrast to recommendations, you may offer and accept endorsements of your skills, which only requires a contact to press a button acknowledging that you have that skill. Because they are so easy to award, endorsements have become somewhat controversial and hold significantly less value than recommendations.

LinkedIn functions as a modern version of a Rolodex® and as a way to keep you in touch with people you know. It also offers you the chance to expand your network by connecting with your contacts' connections. You can connect with those people directly, or you may request introductions to your contacts' connections. In either event, LinkedIn can be a useful way of widening your network.

LinkedIn, which purchased the content sharing platform SlideShare in 2012, also offers opportunities for you to highlight and distribute content you create. You might share blog posts or articles in relevant groups, you might update your status with a mention of an issue you're exploring in an upcoming post, or you might share a PowerPoint presentation desk using SlideShare. Any of these activities allows you to demonstrate and build your credibility, perhaps in the course of building relationships. Be certain that you use a fine touch and some restraint so that your social media activity doesn't become solely focused on sharing your own material, but don't keep your work to yourself. Find the balance between interaction, sharing others' resources, and sharing your own.

If LinkedIn were an in–person gathering, it would be a networking breakfast. You will find people from a variety of industries, holding a variety of positions, all present to conduct business.

Facebook

Facebook began as a social networking tool exclusively for college students, but the average user age as of 2013 is 41, and news reports emphasize that younger users are leaving Facebook for newer (and younger) social media platforms. Unlike LinkedIn, Facebook is designed for social interaction, though more professionals are using it for business purposes as well. You can see and search for people with whom you share a common interest or a common connection, and many users apply a looser standard for accepting "friend requests" on Facebook than they do requests to connect on LinkedIn. Facebook offers a wide variety of applications that permit photo and video sharing, automatic uploading of blog posts, and entertainment.

> ***If Facebook were an in–person gathering, it would be a backyard barbeque.***

You can communicate with another Facebook user by sending her a direct message (private between sender and recipient), by posting on her profile wall (visible to everyone who can see her wall), or by commenting on one of her updates (also visible to everyone who can see her wall). Facebook offers stringent privacy controls, but the standards change on a frequent basis and can be circumvented (intentionally or not) by others. For instance, you may post a photo from a party and restrict it so that only your closest friends see it, but a friend who took a similar shot could post his version and tag you, exposing that image to all of his friends as well as yours.

In comparison to LinkedIn, Facebook is a fairly relaxed online community. People are interested in getting to know one another, but the focus is on the whole person rather than solely on business. If Facebook were an in–person gathering, it might be a backyard barbeque. You will see a wide variety of people attending: some will be off in a corner talking business, some will be sitting around the pool chatting, and some will be playing a game of volleyball. Even when you discuss business on Facebook, you should be aware that your personal friends are nearby (assuming you invited them or let them in the door when they knocked) and that your personal and business contacts can see each other and see what each says about you.

Twitter

Twitter, known as a "microblogging" platform, is probably the most–discussed social media tool available now. Twitter is so popular that it has its own lexicon. According to a late 2008 Pew Internet and American Life Project survey, the median age of a Twitterer (also called a Tweeter) is 31 years old, and some 238 million "tweeple" worldwide are active in the "Twitterverse" or

"Twittersphere" each month, with total accountholders estimate at 883 million. Users send "tweets" of 140 characters or less to share what they are doing or to point their followers to a useful resource. Unlike LinkedIn and Facebook, relationships on Twitter are not reciprocal: tweeter A can follow tweeter B's updates unless B blocks him from doing so, and B will not necessarily follow A's tweets solely because A follows his. You can search for people by name and by interest, and as you start to follow others, you will organically expand the list of people whose updates you find interesting.

> ***If Twitter were an in–person gathering, it might be a quick conversation at the coffee machine.***

Private messages (also limited to 140 characters) may be exchanged between users, and users may respond to one another by including an "@username" at the beginning of a message. The real power of Twitter comes through the potential for messages shared on it to become widespread through "retweets." When a user retweets, she copies your entire message (including your user name) and prefaces it with "RT" (or simply adds quotation marks) and perhaps a comment. She then broadcasts it to all of her followers, who may pick up your message and retweet it themselves, kicking off the start of a viral expansion of your message.

Over time, people will start to get a sense of who you are based on what you find interesting and what you choose to share. Are you talking about other people? Are you talking about events or legal news? Other users will also get an impression of you as they eavesdrop on your Twitter conversations and see what messages (and from whom) you decide to retweet.

If Twitter were an in–person gathering, it might be a quick conversation at the coffee machine. Time (and space) generally prohibit longer conversation, but you would likely find out in brief what your colleagues are working on or if they have seen any interesting news, and they might point you toward a helpful resource or article. As you see who speaks to whom, you identify relationships, and you see who is friendly and willing to help others. Conversation usually starts out somewhat professionally focused, but over time it begins to delve into more personal topics. In this way, you have an opportunity, through quick spurts of conversation, to get to know, like, and trust one another.

Google Plus

Google Plus, or G+, is the newest big social media site gaining momentum. Owned by Google, G+ is growing rapidly and has already surpassed Twitter in number of users worldwide, according to a January 2013 report by Global Web Index.

Similar to Twitter, relationships on Google Plus are not reciprocal. G+ encourages users to follow one another and categorize followers into "Circles." The content shared by any user can be made public or can be shared with specific Circles. This is a useful means of categorizing the people you are connected to and aiming your message, or content, toward certain market segments.

Google Plus differs from Facebook, Twitter and LinkedIn in other ways as well. While communication on Facebook may be more personal, Twitter conversation occurs in short bursts and headlines, and Linkedin is designed for professional interaction, Google Plus posts range from single sentences to full blog post type entries. In fact, some users of G+ use it as a blogging platform, and one "power user" is a photographer who shares his pictures with an audience of more than 5 million people.

G+ also has a feature called Communities. Communities are similar to LinkedIn Groups where people of like mind gather to share insights, ask questions and seek help with issues pertaining to the Community. This particular social networking site also has a built in video conferencing feature called a "hangout" where up to ten people can video and teleconference together in private or public, all free as part of the platform. (Imagine the potential benefit of organizing a panel presentation with virtual face-to-face meetings. Although you might start out as strangers, by the time of the panel, you'd feel that you know one another and would begin your in-person relationship from a higher level.)

What really sets Google Plus apart as a social networking site, however, is the fact that it is owned and run by Google, whose primary function is to deliver search results. Google defines the algorithms used to return results in response to a search request. Because Google Plus is part of the Google Empire, the content shared at G+ is given preferential treatment in search engine results. Google looks through its own network to see if there are any relevant people in your circles or communities that meet your search request. Those results are more likely to be seen as relevant and delivered, often before more influential content. Using Google Plus offers a significant benefit in search engine optimization (SEO), the process you can use to increase the likelihood that your results will be included in response to an appropriate Google search.

Google has also created a Google Plus-based program

called Authorship. Google Authorship takes into account your byline as an "author" on any media you make available on the web. If you have written an article that is published online by a journal, Google Authorship gives you a means to connect that article to your G+ profile, which again enhances search engine results. You can link your G+ profile to your own content as well (on a blog, for instance). This heightened visibility creates a compelling reason to not only use Google Plus but to make sure you are blogging on a regular basis. Together, these two strategies will allow you to be found more often online through searches relevant to your practice.

Other General Social Media Sites

In addition to the "big four" platforms, numerous other social media sites spring up on a regular basis. The latest trend is toward visual media through sites like Pinterest, Instagram, and Vine. Each of these sites allows users to share photos or videos. While it may seem at first blush that such sites are not relevant to a law practice, the question you must ask is whether your ideal clients and referral sources are using those platforms. If so, be creative. You might share infographics relevant to your practice, or you might create short, interesting videos. And in addition to adding visual content that relates to your practice, you might also share some vacation photos, business quotes, or other visuals that reflect on who you are and may help to start or grow a relationship. While these platforms (and the new ones not yet developed) may not be a key part of your marketing, you should keep up to date on the media your audience is adopting and look for ways to use those media.

Lawyer–Specific Social Media

In addition to the many social media platforms that exist for the public at large, certain platforms cater specifically to lawyers. Among these are JD Supra, Law Link, and Legal OnRamp. Each platform offers a unique spin on social media, some providing legal document libraries that users can contribute to and access, others focusing on legal news, and all offering an interactive or networking component. Although each platform has an enthusiastic following, it is simply too early to predict which will prosper over the long term. If your business development plan calls for networking with other lawyers, and if you choose to expand into online networking, you will likely find it beneficial to explore these sites and determine whether they are a fit for you.

Getting Started with Social Media

Entire books have been written about the use of each of the social media platforms discussed in this chapter. The books or training programs recommended on the Rainmaker Resources List (http://www.TheReluctant Rainmaker.com) will ease the time required for you to get started. With the caveat that the suggestions included here are incomplete, these tips will point you in the right direction.

- **Decide strategically which social media platforms to use.** Just because Oprah has finally made an appearance on Twitter does not mean that you should, nor should your colleague's skepticism at the benefits of exchanging 140–character updates mean that you should not. A LinkedIn profile is probably a minimum necessity simply because it has become the *de facto* professional online professional networking platform, and you should not overlook the advantages offered by Google+. You should choose carefully whether to expand your activities further.

- **Create a complete, compelling profile on each service you use, and ensure that your profile matches the site etiquette.** Your LinkedIn profile should closely match your résumé in tone and scope. While the same information may appear on your Facebook profile, you will likely choose less formal language to describe your practice. If you create a profile on Twitter, etiquette suggests that you use an entirely different tone and focus more on your personal interests with a nod to your professional life, rather than the other way around. Because Google+ is so fully user-defined, you may select the style of profile that best fits your practice and your personality.
- **Participate actively on the platforms you select.** While you may find some benefit from simply having a profile, the true utility of social media comes through its use. Share interesting resources, offer help when you see an opportunity, and comment on others' postings. You would not attend an in–person gathering and expect to get great results if you don a name tag and stand just inside the entrance, and the same is true of social media.
- **Remember the "social" part of social media, and do not focus exclusively on yourself.** When you

connect with others, find a way to connect with them in substance as well as in form. Interact with your connections, your friends, or your followers. Otherwise, you run the risk of appearing to be a self–promoter, and few people will be excited about developing a relationship.

- **Use your social media time wisely.** The basic services on most social media platforms are free, and upgraded memberships are relatively inexpensive. The investment demanded by social media is not money, but time. When you have decided how you want to use social media, devise a schedule for your interactions. Most people find that 15 minutes a day or 30 minutes three times a week is sufficient. Regardless of the schedule you set, put some boundaries around your social media time. Online activity can turn into a procrastination tool extraordinaire, and a recent study proved that the most interesting people on social media are those who have busy and fulfilling offline lives that provide fodder for their online activity.
- **Explore applications that allow you to update multiple social media platforms.** If you choose to use LinkedIn, Google+, Facebook, and Twitter, you could spend ten minutes each time you update your status on the four platforms. Instead, try a service like HooteSuite, which allows you to select the platforms on which you would like your posts to appear, including the three already mentioned plus many others. Be sure to consider the propriety of your post for each platform: you might start a great conversation on Twitter by making a humorously derisive comment about a legal or

political development, but such a comment would likely not serve you well if posted on LinkedIn.

- **Consider the impact of your online activity, and consider the potential impact of your contacts' online banter with you.** One interesting by–product of social media is that we have all become much more transparent, blending professional and personal lives in a somewhat seamless online web. Authenticity is a key leadership competency, in that a successful leader will be essentially the same person in every community and situation, though she may call forward different aspects of herself in each. In this way, social media reinforces the opportunity for authenticity. It is quite possible that you could connect with a potential client because you both have the same dry wit and enjoy each other's comments on news. Unfortunately, it is also quite possible for a potentially strong connection to be destroyed by third party comments or postings that reflect poorly on you. Think twice before posting those hilarious photos from your college drinking days online: even if you are not yet connected to professional contacts, you may be so in the future, and professional contacts may uncover your profile through search engines even without being connected. You should be protective of your online appearance and reputation, and you should be careful about the people with whom you connect online.

Social media presents exciting new possibilities for interacting and have great potential for building professional relationships that may lead to business.

Choose and conduct your online activity according to your business development plan, and be mindful of the risks and protection that online activity affords.

The Bottom Line for Reluctant Rainmakers

Participation in social media is not a silver bullet for lawyers seeking to grow their practices. It may be more comfortable for some reluctant rainmakers than in–person networking, and it removes some of the barriers to in–person events, such as travel time and the need to make small talk. Social media can reconnect old acquaintances and create opportunities to make new acquaintances that over time may develop into strong professional relationships. Being active in social media may also create the perception that you are tech–savvy and up–to–date on the latest trends, and active participation can generate traffic for your website. All participants, and especially reluctant rainmakers, must keep a careful eye on the benefit-to-investment ratio to make certain that online activity does not outweigh more profitable tasks. As an adjunct to other approaches, however, social media participation can be a healthy avenue to reach clients, referral sources (including other lawyers), and potential clients.

Chapter 15

Internal Networking and Cross–Selling

For lawyers working in a firm of more than one lawyer, cross–selling is often discussed but less frequently realized as a business development goal. In a cross–selling situation, the firm invites a client to explore other areas of the firm's expertise, in the hope that the client will then bring more of its legal work to the firm. In theory, cross–marketing is an obvious win for the firm. Not only does it recruit more billable work (and, in so doing, remove that work from a competitor firm that might try to cross–sell its own services), but it also gives the client additional contacts at the firm. More contacts may yield a longer client relationship and could even prevent the client from deciding to follow a departing lawyer to a new firm. Less obvious is the win for the individual lawyer, especially a lawyer who fears that someone else might bungle the client's work or one who contemplates the potential of moving to another firm and thus might prefer to encourage personal client loyalty rather than promoting a firm–based relationship.

These individual concerns about cross–selling, along with the common mistakes in business development addressed in Chapter 1, are responsible for firms' low success in cross–marketing efforts. This chapter will show you how to create cross–selling opportunities, how to handle objections, and what to do if your firm implicitly creates a disincentive to cross–selling.

Internal Networking

Internal networking is at the heart of a successful cross–selling effort. To have any reasonable possibility of cross–selling, you and your colleagues must know who in the firm practices what kind of law with which clients. You might stumble into a cross–selling opportunity if a client happens to mention a matter outside the scope of your engagement, but if you are not clear on which lawyer in the firm should be invited in to discuss that matter, you will almost certainly lose the opportunity or fail to impress your client with your knowledge of and recommendation for your colleague. Imagine this scenario:

> ***In a cross–selling situation, the firm invites a client to explore other areas of the firm's expertise, in the hope that the client will bring more of its legal work to the firm.***

While talking about a trade secret litigation matter, the client told Jackie, lead counsel on the matter, that an employee who had been designated as a probable witness could be a problem. On deeper inquiry, Jackie learned that the employee had been terminated and was threatening to sue the company. The client shared that in–house counsel had reviewed the matter and provided some input and planned to retain outside counsel, but no action had been taken. Seizing the opportunity, Jackie asked if the client would like to talk with one of the firm's employment litigators, and the client asked which lawyer she would recommend. Unfortunately, Jackie's mind went blank and although she was able to suggest several lawyers, she was unable to remember any particular success stories to share to bolster their expertise. In fact, she realized partway through the conversation, she had no idea about the scope of those lawyers' practices and could not name a representative client. Her client promised to think about it, and the moment passed—as did the opportunity.

Imagine how different the conversation might have gone if Jackie had responded, "How about if I ask Steve Karran, our resident employment litigation expert, to sit down with us later this afternoon? If I'm not mistaken, he handled a situation recently in which a terminated employee threatened to sue and to 'forget' the information on which she was prepared to testify, and he got the matter settled quickly and on very favorable terms for the client. I'm sure he would be happy to tell you more." By answering that clearly, Jackie would have demonstrated her knowledge of and confidence in her colleague as well as his expertise in the matter under discussion. While it would be impossible to guarantee an outcome, it is easy to imagine that the client might well have responded more favorably to that pitch.

Internal networking is critical for lawyers who have an opportunity to cross–sell, and it is equally important for more junior lawyers who are at the stage to seek assignments. You must know what other lawyers are doing in your firm. You should understand your firm's organization (by departments and practice groups, for example), and you should consider which groups are most likely to have matters of interest to your clients. If your firm is small enough that you can know each person and have some understanding of his practice, so much the better; if not, identify the lawyers who are most active and who are well–regarded, and learn about them first.

Internal networking requires two stages of activity, just as external networking does. Stage I is your homework phase. Read your firm's website, read your colleagues' biographical sketches, and note representative clients and matters. You will not be able to have an encyclopedic knowledge of all work within your firm, of course, but if you can identify and retain a few of the most important pieces of information, you will be armed with the necessary background. Select three to five lawyers or groups whose practices are complementary to your own.

> ***Internal networking is critical for lawyers who have an opportunity to cross–sell, and it is equally important for more junior lawyers who are at the stage to seek assignments.***

When you have completed your homework, shift to Stage II. Talk with the individuals or groups you have selected and explain that you are learning more about their practices so that you will be in a position to refer business to them when an opportunity arises. Especially if you can demonstrate why such an opportunity is likely to occur (if, for example, you have your own book of business), your colleagues will probably be quite happy to share information with you. If your colleagues are amenable, you might even consider setting a regular meeting to discuss cross–selling opportunities. By leading the way, you may prompt others to think about what you might offer to their clients; if not, you can make your offer later.

As you might imagine, the process of internal networking does not end. As with external networking, you will develop close professional relationships with a handful of your colleagues and others will remain at a friendly acquaintance level. Firm populations have a habit of changing, especially given how common lateral moves have become. You will need to stay on top of who is doing what, but you will likely find that incremental education about your colleagues is neither difficult nor unpleasant.

Create Cross–Selling Opportunities

Once you have done your homework and identified a handful of lawyers or groups with practices complementary to yours and laid the groundwork, have a meeting with each to explore possibilities. Be clear that you are exploring how to cross–sell with this lawyer or group. Candor will make some lawyers more likely to meet with you and others less so, but your candor improves the chances of a profitable outcome from any meetings that do occur.

Before your meeting, give thought to your clients and their needs that could possibly be addressed by a lawyer or group that you have selected. What concerns has the client expressed? What do you know about the client's business or industry that may suggest areas of increasing focus? You will probably discover that your client is working with other lawyers in the area in which you have identified potential; if so, what have you been able to determine about your client's level of satisfaction with those lawyers? In short, what could this lawyer or group bring to your client?

Your meeting should give room for consideration of your ideas and for your colleague's reactions and additional thoughts. This is also the time to handle potential objections to cross–selling. If your internal networking has been accomplished with care, the lawyers with whom you discuss cross–selling will probably have come to know, like, and trust you, which should eliminate any fears that you might make a mistake that would ruin their own client relationships or try to steal their clients. You should, nevertheless, bring these common objections to the table and make the case for how cross–selling will benefit the clients, the lawyers involved, and the firm at large.

Your objective for each meeting should be to determine whether the lawyer or group with whom you are speaking is interested in moving forward. If so, you will probably have a conversation with many ideas popping, and the next step is to include the client in the conversation. Again, be transparent in your request: if your client has no desire to explore expanding the scope of the engagement with your firm, better to know on the front end. However, make sure to tell your client that you have been reviewing the representation with colleagues and that your client service team has developed some issues that the client might be interested in discussing. Inform the client that you have already talked about ideas and that this is not the typical "meet'n'greet" designed only to make introductions and to ask the client whether it has any concerns that might be addressed by the lawyers whom you are introducing.

Putting time in before the meeting even occurs should send the client the message that you and the firm are genuinely interested in better serving the client, not interested solely in increasing your billables. Many lawyers interested in cross–selling fail to put the client first in this manner and thus undercut their overture. As always, ask questions, listen closely to the answers, and keep your eye on client service.

Handling Client Objections to Cross–Selling

If you have approached cross–selling with the process suggested above, in which you gather a team of lawyers to explore the client's needs and, most importantly, to listen to what the client has to say about those needs, most objections will be managed organically. The client may have unspoken questions about or objections to retaining your firm to handle another matter, and you should listen closely for any such issues. If any do arise, they will likely be one of the following:

- **The client has worked with another lawyer or firm for quite some time.** Perhaps the client is satisfied with the relationship, in which case the best response you can make would be to request that the client consider you should the other firm ever be conflicted out of a matter or fail to meet the client's expectations.

  On the other hand, the client may be willing to contemplate shifting the work to your firm but may hold back because your firm would need time to get up to speed on the matter. Because a financial concern often underlies the client's reticence, the proposed team should be prepared to explain how it would approach the matter to avoid duplicating costs.

Perhaps you could offer an all–hands meeting at no cost to the client, or you might propose writing off a specified number of hours as the team gets up to speed. Be prepared to address this issue, and you may find that your proposed solution is itself less important than the fact that you have shown economic sensitivity and have considered the issue.

- **The client has some discomfort with your firm or the lawyers proposed to do the work.** If you sense an unspecified reluctance to consider moving a matter to your firm, you might contemplate asking point–blank whether the client has any particular reservations. You might discover concern about other clients whose interests may be competitive to the client's, for example, or you might learn that the client is unconvinced that the approach you suggest is solid. In any event, once you have exposed the reason for the hesitation, you are in a better position to address it.

Regardless of the source or substance of the client's potential objections, try to draw it into open conversation and listen closely to the client's response. You will not be able to address every objection in every case, but exposing the true concerns will give you the best opportunity to do so when possible.

Handling Firm Disincentives to Cross–Selling

Unfortunately, firm disincentives foreclose many cross–selling opportunities. These disincentives take many forms: no expectation that lawyers will cross–sell, less origination credit recognition for expansion of engagements through cross–selling than for new engagements, and variations in the compensation scheme based on client acquisition as opposed to matter acquisition are just a few examples.

If your firm implicitly discourages cross–selling through any of these disincentives, your options may be limited unless you have the political capital to suggest a reevaluation and change in these policies. If not, you may be well–advised to spend your time on expanding your engagements with your own clients, on external rainmaking, and on internal networking for support and referral purposes only.

Before you give up on cross–selling, however, consider whether it might be to your advantage to attempt a cross–selling campaign that would introduce enough, or powerful enough, lawyers to your clients to launch a grassroots movement toward changing the firm culture. Such a movement is unlikely to be quick, however, and if undertaken without the support of firm management or mentors, it is likely to be a frustrating process.

The Bottom Line for Reluctant Rainmakers

Cross–selling straddles the line between business development with your own clients and with strangers. Although your colleagues' clients are strangers to you, you get a credibility boost from your association with your colleagues, whom their clients already know, like, and trust. It would be a mistake to believe that cross–selling is easier than bringing in business from other sources, as should be demonstrated by the numerous objections addressed in this chapter. However, it offers the unique advantages of building additional relationships with a firm client and harnessing as–yet untapped resources within the firm. By doing so, you may strengthen your influence and connections within the firm and create the potential of another referral source through the client now exposed to your work.

Chapter 16

Asking for the Business

If there is a single part of business development that reluctant rainmakers dread the most, the description—even the mention—of which provokes sweaty palms and pounding hearts, it is the moment in which the rainmaker must ask for the business. As soon as the prospect of asking for business comes up, the objections start to stir. "I didn't go to law school to be a salesman." "I don't want to be pushy or obnoxious." "I don't want to seem desperate." "I don't want to offend anyone." Asking for business admittedly can be uncomfortable and difficult. Most lawyers are also savvy enough to recognize the fine line between expressing interest in filling an expressed need (asking for the business, in other words) and soliciting, which is prohibited by ethics rules. No one wants to stray over the line and to look or feel like the proverbial ambulance chaser, always out to sign the client no matter what.

Fortunately, there is another side to the story. As you have no doubt heard in other contexts, "If you don't ask, you don't get." Business development conversations can be awkward in part because both parties are doing a social dance in which one carries the lead for a time and then the other takes over, each trying to probe (among other things) the other party's interest in moving forward with the work and ability to do so. One might infer that interest simply from the fact that the two parties are having the discussion, but multiple other reasons could exist: for example, the prospective client might want to get some free insight into the legal matter or to get information to be used as leverage with another lawyer, and the lawyer might want to be helpful or to get some free insight into business circumstances influencing the matter at hand. It is imperative that you let her know that you would like to handle the matter that you are discussing. Otherwise, though it might seem entirely obvious to you, she might assume that you are not interested.

This chapter will consider three key questions. First, *should* you ask for the business? Second, if so, how do you do so without running afoul of the ethical rules? How should you lead the conversation so that you are prepared to offer to handle the matter? And finally, what language might you use to make the offer?

Should You Ask for the Business?

If you accept that you must express your interest in working with the potential client on the matter that you have been discussing, the first decision you must make is whether to ask for the business. The judgment call is simple but not always easy. After you have explored the matter at hand, the potential client's concerns and objectives, your suggestions on how to approach the situation, and any analogous experience you may have, only one decision remains. Will this client hire you? This is the moment to express interest in handling the matter for the client... Or is it?

Before you make another move, pause to reflect on the conversation. Is this a client you want? Do you want to work on this matter? Most often, the answer will be a clear affirmative. On occasion, though, you may feel some hesitation. If so, you should explore that nagging sense of discomfort and get to the bottom of it. A significant proportion of lawyers representing unpleasant, unrealistic, or unbalanced clients admit that there was something in the initial meetings that should have warned them away from the matter. These kinds of clients are rarely, if ever, satisfied. Representing them is a drag on a practice and may even lead to a bar complaint, which (unfounded or not) will require time and perhaps money to answer. Keep in mind these warning signals to help you avoid undesirable clients:

A significant proportion of lawyers representing unpleasant, unrealistic, or unbalanced clients admit that there was something in the initial meetings that should have warned them away from the matter.

- **The client who has already retained and fired several lawyers.** Some clients have bad experiences with their lawyers and are blameless. The more lawyers a client has retained and fired, however, the more likely that the client is contributing (perhaps significantly) to the problems. Multiple hirings and firings on a single matter is a clear warning, but serial representations over time can indicate a problem, a preferred lawyer who has switched firms several times, or simple business preference. If you discover that the prospective client has worked with multiple lawyers or law firms over a short period of time, ask plenty of questions about what the lawyers did well and poorly. The information you get will help you if you work with the client, and it may steer you away from a troublesome situation.

- **The unrealistic client.** Especially among clients who are not legally sophisticated, you may find that expectations are out of line with realistic results. The important factor is how the potential client responds to the adjustment. Does she continue to press her demand and to ignore your warning?

  Jennifer, a sole practitioner with a concentration in labor and employment law, consulted with a prospective client who was terminated from her position because of online activity that the employer considered an unsavory reflection on the company. The potential client had received Jennifer's name from a former client who successfully maintained a complaint for sex discrimination and received a substantial settlement. Because of her own experience, the former client recommended that the prospective client hold out for a settlement of $1 million, which Jennifer considered completely unrealistic. The prospective client would not budge, and Jennifer elected not to take the case. She later heard through the grapevine that her potential client had hired another lawyer, received a settlement in the tens–of–thousands of dollars range, and filed a bar complaint for malpractice. Jennifer was grateful to have avoided that problem.

- **The client who pushes on fees.** Almost everyone, lawyers included, experiences a sense of sticker shock upon discovering the cost of engaging a lawyer. Some clients may request a discount, payment terms of some sort, a fee cap, or another method of limiting the potential fee exposure. Others, however, try to chip away at the estimate and reduce it in any way possible. Ask yourself how much haggling you expect from a prospective client. If you have the sense that this client will push back on every expense, question every bill, and drag out payment, you may decide not to take the case. Especially if the case is relatively small, fee pressure can eliminate any profit on a matter, and the process of dealing with the client may be sufficiently unpleasant that you would prefer not to bother.

- **The client who is hard to pin down.** This kind of potential client may reveal himself in a variety of ways, such as changing the date for your meeting several times, missing the meeting entirely but calling later to apologize profusely, changing the focus of the conversation, or changing his explanation of the situation. If you get a gut sense that something does not add up with a prospective client's behavior, pay close attention.

- **The rude client.** Some clients will be rude to your staff and perfectly appropriate with you, and others will be rude to everyone. Whether limited or widespread, continuous rudeness will make life unpleasant for you and your staff.

- **The overly demanding client.** Sometimes an emergency is legitimate, but if you (or your staff) sense that a prospective client is pushing unduly for an appointment, beware. Clients who demand to speak with you immediately, as if their matter is the only matter you are handling, often have unrealistic expectations of how an engagement should run. Sometimes those expectations are limited to communication, but frequently the demands expand in other ways as well.

If you sense a problem with a prospective client, do not simply ignore it. Sometimes the problem can be overcome by working to manage the client's expectations. In other instances, after exploring the situation, you will decide that the proposed engagement is more trouble than it is worth. If you fail to acknowledge and consider whatever information troubles you during a consultation, you may find yourself spending inappropriate amounts of time and energy that could have been avoided.

If you decide that you do want to work with the potential client, you must still determine whether to ask explicitly for her business. You may pick up some clues through the conversation about whether the potential client expects a request for the business. If not, as is probably more likely, you should weigh the likelihood that the request will be accepted. Based on general counsel interviews conducted for this book, a significant number of clients do not want a lawyer to ask overtly for the business in a way that demands a yes-or-no response. Some in–

house lawyers felt put on the spot; others simply did not like to have to tell the requesting lawyer that the potential client would be placing or leaving its work with another lawyer. Whether you choose a direct approach or a more oblique offer, however, you must express your interest in the client and the matter.

How Do You Avoid Running Afoul of the Ethics Rules?

Having decided to express interest in representing a prospective client, the question becomes how to express interest and ask for the business without crossing ethical boundaries. To set the boundary you must not cross, consult the ethical guidelines applicable in your jurisdiction. For discussion purposes, the most common formulation of the anti–solicitation rule of the ABA Model Code of Professional Conduct provides as follows:

Rule 7.3 Direct Contact With Prospective Clients

(a) A lawyer shall not by in–person, live telephone or real–time electronic contact solicit professional employment from a prospective client when a significant motive for the lawyer's doing so is the lawyer's pecuniary gain, unless the person contacted:

(1) is a lawyer; or

(2) has a family, close personal, or prior professional relationship with the lawyer.[3]

---

[3] Note that the rules in your jurisdiction may not follow the ABA Model Code of Professional Conduct.

Based on this common language, you may not explicitly solicit a potential client to give you business unless the potential client is a lawyer, a former client, or family or a close friend. The rules leave significant latitude, however, if you are talking with in–house counsel or a former client. A direct request for business might fall within the ethical guidelines even if made to a college friend with whom you have kept in reasonably close touch, though you would be well–advised to explore ethics opinions issued in your state if you go in a gray area of the rule's application.

You will not find it difficult to stay within the ethical rules prohibiting solicitation as long as you are mindful of the role played by the person with whom you are speaking. Assuming that you are talking with someone whom you may directly solicit under the applicable ethics rules, you must find the right words.

Leading the Conversation

Before you move to asking for the business, either directly or obliquely, be sure that you have helped the client through the process of fully describing the matter needing resolution. Ask open–ended questions to help you appreciate the scope of the issue, the potential client's concerns and considerations, any feedback that the client has received from other sources, and the objectives set for the matter. When you are certain that you fully understand the potential client's needs, you may move into sharing your perspective on the matter as described and your experience in related matters.

Before hiring a lawyer, clients generally want to know that you have the necessary expertise and experience. You might provide lists of representative clients and matters (if not included on your biographical sketch) or case studies, either at the meeting or, if no hiring decision is at hand, as follow–up written material. If other lawyers would be involved in the representation, be sure to highlight their experience and qualifications as you discuss analogous matters the firm has handled. Clients also want to be comfortable with the legal team assembled. If circumstances permit, you might bring in the other lawyers for an introduction, or you could arrange a later meeting. Even if no immediate introduction is possible, weave the other lawyers' experience into your comments. By doing so, you telegraph the message that the other lawyers are an integral part of the team, and you convey your comfort with and confidence in their abilities.

If the matter is sufficiently well–defined, you might move on to propose a few possible courses of action. Although you should include the *caveat* that options and strategic preferences might change as the matter develops, clients will generally appreciate having your view of the approaches that might be considered. Before you lay out any steps, however, you should restate the prospective client's objectives as you perceive them. Doing so will reassure the client that you are careful to understand what is most important in the course of the representation and will give you the opportunity to provide the client with an experience of what it is like to work with you.

To suggest possible avenues for the representation, use conditional language ("if we were to move forward, we could do ABC, which based on what we know now would likely have the effects of XYZ, and that in turn meets the objectives that you've described about PQR") and check with the potential client at each juncture. Ask questions, outline decision points and the likely results, and project consequences. By conducting the conversation in this way, you demonstrate the way you would approach the matter, and most importantly you demonstrate the respect you would show for the client's role in the engagement.

In the course of this conversation, you will likely get a sense of how involved the client would expect to be in the engagement. Moreover, you will begin to understand how the client thinks about the matter, what overarching goals or worries impact how the client will agree to proceed, and whether other decision–makers may weigh in on the hiring decision or on the matter itself. This information will be invaluable if you move forward.

The potential client may ask about your fees or a cost estimate after you have discussed how the matter might proceed. If not, you should raise the issue. Doing so demonstrates that you recognize the importance of financial considerations and that you are comfortable discussing the economics of the client relationship. You might lead into that conversation by asking, "Would it be helpful to discuss what it might cost to move along the lines we have discussed?"

What Language Might You Use to Make the Offer?

Finally, having discussed the matter, your relevant experience, and how you might proceed with the engagement, the conversation will probably reach a natural pause. At that point, you could ask if the prospective client has any additional questions. If not, this is your opportunity to express interest in being awarded the engagement. The words you choose to express your interest or to ask directly for the business must be authentic and reasonably comfortable for you. If not, you may find yourself struggling to get the words out, or you may continue talking after you have made the request to defuse your discomfort. Consider this list of requests, ranging from most oblique to most direct, and ask how you might adapt the language so it fits your style:

The words you choose to express your interest or to ask directly for the business must be authentic and reasonably comfortable for you.

- If you have not had a full discussion about a potential approach) Would you like me to suggest an approach for this based on our conversation and any documents you would like me to review?
- Would you like me to prepare a proposal based on our conversation today?
- (After discussing some possible approaches to the matter at hand) Do any of these approaches feel like a good fit for you?
- (In the same instance) Which approach feels like the right one for you?
- Based on what we have talked about today, would you be interested in moving forward?
- When would you like to move forward with this?
- Is there anyone else with whom I should speak about moving forward?

- Please let me know if I can help you in any way with this issue.
- I would be delighted to work with you on this matter if I can be of assistance.
- If you decide that you would like to move forward on this matter, please let me know.
- May I handle this matter for you?

Each of these business–seeking questions takes a slightly different approach, and you will likely discover a handful that best fit your style. When you have made the request, be quiet. You may receive an objection, a delay tactic, or an acceptance. If you receive an objection, continue to ask open–ended questions to isolate the reason for the objection. If the prospective client expresses discomfort with the options that you outlined for moving forward, you could move back into the "next steps" part of the conversation to clarify the client's goals and concerns.

If there is a financial or timing issue (if, for instance, the potential client references a budgeting issue), isolate the problem and respond as clearly as possible. If feasible, you should go into a potential client meeting with a few ideas about possible alternative billing arrangements, and you should approach that conversation from a mutual problem–solving perspective. Regardless of the nature of the specific objection raised, your task is to listen, to clarify as needed, and to respond non–defensively and in a way that invites collaboration.

If the potential client indicates that a decision must wait for some reason, suggest setting an appointment to check in with the client in the future. To do so, ask how much time the client expects to need to make a decision and suggest a date for further conversation. Setting a future appointment for further conversation will allow you to follow up with the prospective client without feeling as if you are chasing him. If you can secure the client's agreement to a date and time, you have a reasonably good indication that the client is at least considering your proposal. If not, you might ask directly whether the potential client feels that further conversation would be useful.

At a minimum, request that the client tell you whether the steps you have discussed seem to be a fit with the direction she has in mind. If not, you might resurrect the conversation and adjust your suggestions accordingly, if appropriate. Your goal is to leave the meeting, if not with a commitment to proceed, then with a strong sense of the prospective client's genuine interest.

If the client accepts your proposal, congratulations! Your focus must shift immediately to providing stellar client service, as discussed in Chapter 2. Otherwise, be prepared to continue the conversation, to provide helpful resources about the matter at hand or about your (or your firm's) relevant experience, or simply to check with the prospective client to reiterate your understanding of the matter's importance and your desire and ability to help.

The Bottom Line for Reluctant Rainmakers

By following the recommended process (ensuring that you understand the matter at hand and the potential client's objectives and concerns, giving the client a taste of what it would be like to work with you, then asking for the business), you have a checklist–based approach to the sometimes–delicate conversation that may lead to an engagement. When you know what you must do to "close" the conversation, you have more freedom to engage with the potential client on a solution–oriented level. Operating from that perspective often relieves reluctant rainmakers from the sense that they must sell an unwilling potential client.

PART III

Rainmaker Profiles:

Specific Suggestions for Specific Situations

Chapter 17

Years 1–15 in Practice: Seniority–based Rainmaking Tasks for Mid–Sized and Large Firm Lawyers

While any lawyer can use the rainmaker activities discussed in Part II of this book, lawyers in mid–sized and large firms will likely discover that their seniority will dictate the most appropriate tasks for them. Junior associates are often lulled into inaction by the belief that they are too junior to do any sort of business development, while more advanced lawyers sometimes fail to move from the tasks that were appropriate earlier in their career to those more fitting their advanced expertise and experience. This chapter is designed to prescribe tasks for mid–sized and large firm lawyers based primarily on seniority. Mid–sized and large firms are at the heart of this discussion, though it may be applicable to some smaller firms as well, depending on the type of practice and the firm's culture.

In general, larger firms tend to represent larger clients,

mostly on larger matters or a consistent stream of smaller matters, usually with larger bills. Junior associates tend to take on a supporting role, learning how to practice while they learn the law, and in theory these associates will get more client service experience and client contact as they advance. Unlike sole practitioners who, regardless of the complexity of the matters they handle, must take on client development work immediately lest their time in practice be cut short for lack of billable work, larger firm lawyers are often discouraged from participating in any kind of client development activity in the early years of practice.

> ***Only one factor is sufficient to place a lawyer well within the employment "zone of safety": the ability to generate new business.***

Too many lawyers accept the perception that business development activity is not expected of them right up to the point when business development capability becomes a minimum expectation for partnership, or until they make a lateral move to a new firm and discover that rainmaking is a part of their job expectations. For the truly unfortunate, the importance of business development does not become apparent until they want to make a lateral move at some point past the prime midlevel years and discover that they are unable to do so without a book of business.

Even more senior lawyers who have devoted energy to client development are not immune. Senior associates have a buffer of sorts, trying their hand at rainmaking with the perceived security of continuing to receive assignments from partners to maintain their workload. That buffer is, however, deceptive. Client development success or potential is usually considered to be a critical factor in electing a lawyer to partnership. Moreover, successful senior associates elected to partnership may quickly discover that the rules have changed. Being a service partner, one who works on matters brought to the firm by a rainmaker partner, is a precarious position. Indeed, even before the economic crisis of 2008–2009, firms instituted non–equity partnership status, which reflects in financial and political markers the reality that not all partners are equal: those who bring in business are, by far, more important than those who merely do the work, no matter how highly technically demanding the work may be. And despite the fact that they often have employment contracts and are less "expendable" than associates, non–equity partners who are not clearly on track to make the jump to equity partnership are among the least secure law firm employees. Less secure still are those equity partners with a small, unprofitable, or decreasing book of business.

A triumvirate of skills is required for any law firm lawyer. Whether you want to advance at your firm and become the now–rare lawyer who stays with a single firm throughout his career or whether you want to make as many lateral moves as may prove to be advantageous, you must develop these three skills:

1. **Technical legal skill**
2. **Client service skills that enable you to become a trusted advisor**
3. **Business development skill**

Although most larger law firms do a good job of training lawyers in legal skill, client service and business development skills sometimes receive short shrift. The following sections are designed to assist lawyers at the junior, midlevel/senior associate, and new partner levels in finding the right approach to business development.

Beyond the new partner years (roughly a partner's first five years, whether at non–equity or equity status), the trajectory calls basically for more of the same with adjustment over time for rebalancing of administrative, rainmaking, and billable hours.

The Junior Associate

If lawyers have learned anything following the economic difficulties and layoffs of 2009, it must be that even large law firms are not secure. In truth, positions with larger firms historically were no more immune than other kinds of employment, but at least until the "up or out" years, they seemed safe, and associates could feel a sense of security. Then the perfect storm hit: bloated associate salaries, increased billing rates to make up for the high salaries, clients unhappy about paying those increased rates for the most junior associates, and finally the economic downturn and credit crunch. Suddenly, larger law firm associates began to feel that they were standing on shifting sands. In the midst of all this turmoil, only one factor is sufficient to place a lawyer well within the employment zone of safety: the ability to generate new business. With that ability, the lawyer has a practice and profession that he may carry to another firm or into his own practice; without it, the lawyer merely has a job, and lawyers lose jobs every day for reasons both within and outside their control.

Because larger firms tend to handle high–value cases and clients tend to be unwilling to entrust their high–value cases to lawyers without much experience, junior and, in some fields, midlevel associates often feel that they are unable to engage in meaningful business development activity. They recognize that they are unlikely to land a new client or gain responsibility for a new matter from an existing client. Instead of trying to bring in business, they focus on becoming excellent technicians with the hope that one day, sometime down the line, they will advance enough in seniority to become viable rainmakers or to inherit clients from a senior lawyer.

It is true that, in most cases, clients will not turn over substantial matters to junior lawyers. And to be effective lawyers, junior associates must spend the bulk of their time learning the law, both in substance and in practical application. Unfortunately, too many lawyers collapse those truths into the conclusion that junior lawyers therefore cannot engage in rainmaking. Even worse, the widespread acceptance of that conclusion is responsible for the number of associates who expect to begin business development activities no earlier than their midlevel years.

> ***You must not wait until the firm declares that it is time for rainmaking to begin.***
>
> ***Start now.***

Imagine an associate named Patricia, who concentrates entirely on making her billable hours and learning the law, choosing not to take part in the activities that would form a solid foundation for rainmaking because she considers herself "too junior." She will spend, on average, about five years focusing on the law and then will have an awakening that she must learn to build a book of business. If Patricia is lucky, she will recognize that truth herself as she contemplates making partner or developing a practice that she enjoys over which she has substantial control. If she is unlucky, she will learn the truth when she finds the door to partnership closed, when she is laid off, or when she wants to make a lateral move and discovers that she is unable to do so without some track record of business development ability.

Moreover, because the cases at Patricia's large firm are typically high dollar–value, the firm's clients will entrust those matters only to lawyers with significant experience in the field and in whom the clients have confidence. But that confidence does not necessarily develop organically. It springs from getting to know the lawyer, seeing that person in action in several different settings, and having conversations that allow the lawyer to demonstrate legal ability, judgment, and leadership. Developing confidence in a lawyer takes time.

The consequence of all of this is that when Patricia, who has refrained from business development activities, is at last ready to begin rainmaking, she will face a gap of time between the commencement of those activities and reaping the fruits of her labors. Though Patricia is skilled in the law and capable of shepherding a matter, she will have no contacts willing to entrust a matter to her. In other words, she will be ripe to begin taking responsibility for her own clients and matters but because she has not yet engaged in business development activities, no one knows that she is ready.

Because Patricia began to engage in the strategic client contact that produces confidence so late in her career, she is likely to find herself six or more years into her practice before she begins to develop the relationships that may lead to new business. Highly compensated but lacking a book of business or a demonstrated ability to bring in new billable work, Patricia will likely be on the list of layoff candidates if the firm's economic circumstances take a downturn, and she will have trouble securing a new position.

The solution, obviously, is for associates to begin rainmaking activity as soon as possible. More and more large firms are offering business development training to midlevel and even some junior associates, but they rarely offer substantial training before an associate's fifth year. By that time, the problems that Patricia experienced have probably already developed. You must not wait until the firm declares that it is time for rainmaking to begin. Start now.

Junior associates need to begin business development activities from the very beginning of their careers, focusing primarily on credential– and credibility–enhancing activity and secondarily on relationship–building activity. Over time, the emphasis will shift (but not move entirely) to relationship–building activity. Whether you are focusing on credentials or relationships, as a junior associate you should expect to spend about two hours per week on rainmaking activity.

Credential– and Credibility–Enhancing Activity

Junior associates' biographical sketches are often limited to law school experience and a statement of their area of practice, which usually matches their departmental assignment. In other words, a junior associate is more likely to describe himself as an "intellectual property lawyer focusing on patent litigation" than a "patent litigator with special expertise representing generic pharmaceutical companies in Hatch–Waxman matters." Because proficiency results from numerous experiences over time, of course, junior associates' inability to claim high skill in a specific area of the law is not surprising.

However, if an associate seeks out writing

opportunities (likely in conjunction with a partner) and bar association or relevant industry organization committee work, he has an opportunity to develop expertise more quickly than he will if he relies only on billable work to grow. It can be surprisingly simple to achieve positions of some responsibility on committees, and those positions enhance not only actual legal knowledge but also others' perception of the associate's knowledge and skill. Whether the resulting work is a report to a larger body, an article published in the organization's newsletter or journal, or an oral presentation, the associate who is involved in that activity garners exposure within the field and an item to add to his biographical sketch.

Within a few years of getting involved in writing and bar or industry association committee work, invitations to speak often follow. Client engagements rarely flow directly from any of these activities, but taking part in them will permit you to begin growing a reputation for expertise and involvement in the field of your choice. Committee work, in particular, also puts you in contact with others in your field of interest and allows you to begin building relationships.

Relationship–Building Activity

Relationships are critical for business development, because trust and confidence grow as relationships develop. Junior associates have three primary opportunities to begin building relationships that will, in time, have a good likelihood of yielding new business.

- **Maintain connections with law school classmates**. Most students regard law school as the final chapter of their education when in fact it is the first chapter of their professional career. Classmates are future colleagues. After graduation and over the years, classmates will scatter to various firms and into corporate positions. At first, of course, everyone will be quite junior. But over time, former classmates will advance in their own careers, and maintaining connections creates the opportunity to learn about legal needs and to be known as a resource for fulfilling them. You will find it beneficial to keep in touch with former classmates on at least an annual or semi–annual basis, and you might even consider serving as your class's alumni contact. You might be asked to take part in activities like signing fundraising letters and attending alumni meetings, providing opportunities for contact with classmates with whom you would probably otherwise lose touch completely. Though you should analyze the probable cost/benefit ratio before agreeing to take on time–intensive activities, such roles can be helpful for creating one–on–one contact and can also elevate you to visibility that leverages your time by keeping your name in front of a group of potential referral sources on a regular basis.

Most students regard law school as the final chapter of their education when in fact it is the first chapter of their professional career.

Ideally, you will also keep in touch with law students you met during your summer associate work, college classmates, and even some high school classmates. Most students in college forget to consider the value that longstanding connections may bring, and so it is common that lawyers keep in touch with only a handful of friends from pre–law school days. If that is your situation, you might consider attending alumni functions to dip back into your college classmate pool. The closer you are to your college days, the easier your opportunity to reestablish friendships. As with law school classmates, your college classmates will begin their careers in junior positions (though some who moved directly into the corporate world will have a several-year head start on you), but they will advance in their careers. You will likely be a valuable resource as your non–lawyer college contacts begin to encounter legal questions, and especially if you devote strategic consideration to growing certain relationships, you may find that business will result over the years.

- **Get to know others through committee work**. By working actively within bar association or industry committees, associates begin to make connections with others who are on a peer level as well as with more senior professionals. Mentoring opportunities may arise, and you may build relationships characterized by trust and mutual respect. In time, those relationships may yield referrals or direct engagements.

You must consider which committees and what kind of activity will be beneficial for you. Chapter 9 offers general suggestions for committee work, but additional factors are at play for junior associates. Unlike more senior lawyers, you will likely need to serve a few years before you have the experience or opportunity to move into leadership positions in bar or industry organizations.

As a result, you should consider selecting the committees with which you get involved not on the basis of the likelihood of a quick transition into leadership but instead on the basis of the other committee members with whom you will work. If, for instance, you have an opportunity to work on a committee with someone who is regarded as a thought leader in the relevant area, that contact could benefit you with an increase in your substantive knowledge, enhanced understanding of the key players in the area, and insight into how to think about various issues. Personal contact with luminaries brings other benefits as well, such as introductions to other top achievers or information about professional opportunities. For junior associates, with whom you work may be just as important as (and perhaps even more important than) the subject area in which you work.

- **Stay in contact with client peers**. Very often, in corporate representations, senior associates and partners will have primary client contact and will be responsible for communicating with the C–level corporate representatives and decision makers. However, even junior associates typically have some client contact with more junior representatives. Many associates overlook the fact that, just as they will advance from junior to midlevel to senior associate, their client-contact peers will also advance in responsibility. Those contacts may move from the current client

> organization to another, and long–standing business relationships that began when the corporate representative and lawyer were both quite junior may yield new client engagements.

If you have client contact with someone at your peer level, consider how you can develop that relationship. Look for opportunities to follow up with that contact as discussed throughout this book, and make sure that you keep in touch with her even after the legal engagement has ended. Contact all of your peer–level client contacts at least twice each year—perhaps by sending a holiday card and by scheduling coffee or a check-in telephone call at least once—and make sure that you find out when they move to a new position. Offer feedback and resources. Some peer contacts will change fields or otherwise move out of the sphere of your typical strategic rainmaking contact profile, but you would be wise to continue passive contact (by holiday card, personalized but generic note, and the like) anyway. During the course of a representation, it is likely that your contact will come to know, like, and trust you—and vice versa—and even if that person then moves into an unrelated field, you should never squander that kind of connection.

For junior associates, with whom you work may be just as important as the subject area in which you work.

By beginning credential– and credibility–enhancing activity as soon as possible (ideally, within the first two years of practice) and by continuing to build relationships that began in law school (and, preferably, even those from college and before), junior associates in larger firms can create a solid foundation for future business development. Midlevel associates may begin taking part in additional rainmaking activities and participating in client development, and those activities will be much more successful if they are layered onto a base of technical legal expertise and credentials that reflect that expertise, appreciation of the importance of business development, and relationships built over time.

Get the Information You Need to Succeed

As a junior associate at a large firm, it is unlikely that anyone will raise business development as an item for your "to do" list. You can, however, take the initiative and put yourself in line for mentorship and training as soon as possible by inquiring about opportunities to learn. Search out a mentor who is a rainmaker in your firm and let that person know you want to learn how to follow in her footsteps. Especially if you acknowledge that you are unlikely to bring in new business in the short term but that long–term success depends on your early attention to rainmaking, a mentor may appreciate your enthusiasm and foresight.

A business development mentor will guide you not only in general principles of business development but also in your firm's specific cultural expectations. You will learn "how we do it here" and will, in the process, develop a powerful ally. And by seeking out a strong mentor and showing enthusiasm for learning the art of client development, you will likely set yourself apart from your more passive peer–level colleagues who are content to wait until the firm offers business development training.

Whom should you select as a mentor? If you can identify someone (preferably in your practice area) who is well–regarded for developing new business, you need inquire no further. Age, gender, and background are far less important than business development ability, and because a lawyer's standing in the firm will most often be tied (at least in part) to rainmaking ability, someone who is a rainmaker will almost always be a good choice politically regardless of other attributes.

> ***By seeking out a strong mentor and showing enthusiasm for learning client development, you will set yourself apart from your more passive colleagues who are content to wait until the firm offers training.***

Meet with your mentor at least once a quarter, and make it your business to study what your mentor does and to find ways in which you might contribute to his successful activity, perhaps by sharing relevant resources or skill. Your in–firm mentor should not be your only resource for learning about business development, but he will be a key resource within your firm.

In addition, schedule a meeting with your in–house business development personnel to find out what they do. Some firms have systems through which a lawyer may propose articles and request that a staff member pitch the article to various publications so she knows before she begins writing when and where an article will be published. Make it a point to find out about any such resources your business development personnel may offer. Enthusiasm will carry you a long way with these staff members, especially since so many lawyers detest business development and make the marketing team's objectives more difficult to meet as a result.

Find out whether the firm provides a business development budget and, if so, what you need to do to access it. Must you put in a request before purchasing tickets for a sporting event, for example? Are you required to provide a report following an out-of-town seminar or organization's meeting so that the firm can evaluate whether the activity produced sufficient benefit to be repeated in the future? Every firm has different standards. If your firm has none, ask your rainmaker mentor what she would recommend you do to build a good record of purposeful and strategic business development activity.

Beginning business development activity is critical, as is ensuring that the activities you choose are an appropriate match to your level of seniority. Demonstrate enthusiasm and strategic planning, find a mentor, and set goals and milestones to ensure that you stay on track with your professional development as well as your business development. If you begin these activities early, you will have a solid foundation upon which to build by the time you hit your midlevel years, and you will dramatically increase the opportunities available to you as your career progresses.

The Midlevel or Senior Associate

By the time you have reached your midlevel or senior associate years, you will have built a firm foundation of legal knowledge. Though you will always have more to learn as the law evolves, you will feel comfortable with a wide variety of matters within your practice area, and you will know how to approach ancillary issues as well, including when to reach out to another lawyer for specialized assistance.

Clients are probably more comfortable with you now, and some may even seek you out for advice. You probably have one or two articles in print, perhaps more if you have been industrious, and you likely have an established network composed of former classmates, former colleagues, perhaps midlevel and senior client (or former client) representatives, and others with whom you have crossed professional paths. If not, your immediate task is to do some remedial work (see the Junior Associate section *supra*).

Whereas junior associates should be spending an average of two hours a week on business development activity, your time investment should be between three and four hours per week. If you have engaged in article–writing in the past, evaluate where your articles have been published and what results (if any) can be traced to the publication. Articles written collaboratively between associates and partners usually feature the partner's name first, and if you have not yet authored an article under your own name, you should do so now. Seek out opportunities to deliver speeches or seminars in your area of practice, by yourself or as a member of a panel. When you appear live before an audience, you have an opportunity not only to enhance your credentials but also to develop a rapport with audience members. Making presentations offers a natural segue from credential–building activity to relationship–building activity.

Midlevel and senior associates should engage in significant internal networking, building relationships with partners, and growing a reputation as a capable colleague. These connections will be useful if you consider making a lateral move, if you are up for a partnership vote, and for long–term business development opportunities. In addition, you should look to expand your external networking based upon your business development plan.

Remember to stay in touch with client representatives at your peer level, particularly as their career paths take them to new organizations. As you move into your midlevel and senior associate years, you should explore more specific networking opportunities within your client industries. For instance, if you practice environmental law and work with clients who are architects, you should look for environmental organizations with a substantial number of members who are architects or architectural organizations with an environmental focus.

Midlevel and senior associates should engage in significant internal networking, building relationships with partners, and growing a reputation as a capable colleague.

Although you may not yet be responsible for client engagements (and have most likely not signed a client yet), your client contact should be steadily increasing. One challenge that some associates experience as they advance in seniority is working with lawyers who prefer to protect client contact as if they literally own the relationship. That approach tends to be short–sighted. Clients are often more comfortable in a representation when they can call more than a single lawyer and feel confident that they are receiving good counsel, and a strong client service team will usually strengthen the bond between a client and her lawyer's law firm. In today's portability–focused atmosphere, however, some lawyers would prefer to keep a one–on–one personal relationship with their clients so that clients will feel little hesitation before following their lawyer to a new firm. This proclivity can be further encouraged by firms' compensation structure, as well.

What if you are working for a partner who has not encouraged you to build a relationship with the clients you are serving? You must respect the partner's preference and should not attempt to create a relationship without his approval. However, you might suggest at least meeting the client, so that you could better support the client should the partner be out of the office. If the partner has simply not considered your potential as a rainmaker, taking the initiative may increase your opportunities by creating the possibility in the partner's mind.

In addition, you should look for ways to make the partner look good to the client by offering useful resources to the partner for his delivery to the client. When you show that your goal is to provide superior client service, the partner may become more comfortable involving you in client meetings and helping you to build a relationship with his clients. You may, despite your best efforts, be unsuccessful in acquiring substantial client contact in some relationships. If that proves true, make sure that you provide top–notch service as you complete billable work for those clients. While pure work will not substitute for a relationship, it may lay the groundwork for a future relationship, should circumstances change.

Finally, by the time you are a senior associate, you should be comfortable with the process of evaluating the likelihood of future engagements or referrals through a contact, and you should know how to ask. Review Chapter 16 and practice with your mentor, coach, or business development accountability group so that you know what to say and how. Even selecting a simple question such as, "Would you consider referring me to your contact?" can be enough to move a relationship forward. You may not yet be at the stage to ask for an engagement, but you should look for opportunities to request referrals in a mutually–beneficial relationship with other professionals. The more secure you become offering assistance and requesting permission to move forward with a representation, the more effective you will be when the opportunities to do so arise.

The New Partner

Common wisdom holds that the first few years of partnership are among the leanest, most difficult years of a lawyer's practice. If you are elected as an equity partner directly from the associate or of counsel ranks, you will see your responsibilities increase and you may see your compensation decrease. If you are elected as a non–equity partner, you have another few years of proving yourself before you have a chance to become an equity partner, and although you may have an employment contract that provides some job security, you may also find yourself in a perilous no–man's land between associate and equity partner. In either case, your new partners will be looking to you to generate new work, and you may find that fewer senior partners are inclined to staff you on cases they brought to the firm. That reluctance may stem from fear of losing a client to you, from desire to pass the work on to more junior lawyers for economic reasons, or from the sense that you have now "grown up" enough to be responsible for bringing in your own work.

If you have followed the suggestions for senior associates, this transition may require less adjustment in terms of rainmaking tactics and more in terms of time management. You are likely to find your time at a higher premium as you are assigned new administrative duties and as your business development activities swell to require five to six hours each week. Review Part IV for suggestions on how to prioritize your tasks, and make sure that you place rainmaking activity at the top of your "to do" list.

Stay on top of the practices maintained within your firm, identify practice groups complementary to your own, and know as much as you can about the individual lawyers in those groups.

Continue your internal business development work. As a partner, you may have opportunities for cross–selling, or you may be able to create those opportunities. (See Chapter 15 for a full discussion of cross–selling.) You must know your colleagues and their practice areas to cross–sell effectively, and you must find ways to stay top–of–mind with lawyers whose practices complement yours. A daunting task in a mid–sized firm, you may find it impossible to know all of your colleagues in a large firm. If your firm is large enough that it is not possible to develop some relationship with all of your colleagues, identify the practice groups most likely to have a synergy with your practice, and devote yourself to getting to know those lawyers.

You must have a strong sense of what practice areas your colleagues maintain so that you can quickly and confidently advise a contact whether your firm can handle a particular matter. Ideally, you would be able to identify the person who is skilled in a requested practice and to offer an introduction, but that level of facility may be impossible if your firm size hits triple digits. Make it your habit to stay on top of the practices maintained within your firm, to identify practice groups complementary to your own, and to know as much as you can about the individual lawyers in those groups.

Finally, as a partner, you may now have access to junior associates who can assist you with writing and preparing presentations. You can make effective use of your time and resources by creating opportunities to speak and for publication through your networking activity and working with more junior lawyers who can carry a large part of the load. Some associates may complain (indirectly, if not to you) about taking on a non–billable project, but a smart lawyer will recognize the benefits if you mentor her through research and product preparation, thus helping her to increase her knowledge of the law. You may choose to include her as a co–author or to acknowledge her contribution, thus lending her some of your credibility and giving her a credential for her biographical sketch.

By approaching your writing and speaking tasks this way, you are able to leverage your time, continuing to grow your list of writing and speaking accomplishments while spending most of your energy on relationship–centered tasks, and benefiting a more junior lawyer as well.

Chapter 18

Sole and Small Firm Practitioners

A small firm or sole practitioner's business development role is similar to that of a large firm lawyer, except that the sole practitioner must fulfill all roles—junior/midlevel/senior associate and partner—all at the same time, often without the resources available to large firm lawyers. In a sense, Ann Richards' commentary on gender differences is equally applicable to the difference between solo lawyers and large firm lawyers: "Ginger Rogers did everything Fred Astaire did, except backwards and in high heels." Daunting, no doubt, but sole practitioners do have advantages that large firm lawyers lack. (Even though you are not working in a large firm, reading Chapter 17 pertaining to large firm lawyers will give you significant insight into the approaches you need to take and how to go about establishing the credibility and connections necessary for your practice to thrive.)

Small firms often incorporate certain habits of larger firms and others more common to sole practitioners. The firm culture determines whether one of the models is dominant or whether a mix applies. If you are a small firm lawyer, review Chapter 17 and this chapter and note which set of steps seems most applicable to your practice. Although the remainder of this chapter focuses exclusively on sole practitioners, be aware that the comments apply equally to those in small firms who practice as if the firm is a confederation of sole practitioners.

The chief advantage of being a sole practitioner is that you have full responsibility for setting the course of your practice, based only on your preferences and your business judgment. You have no partners to issue directions or to quash your plans, and your rainmaking opportunities are entirely self–directed. Although individual business development success is equally important for sole practitioners and those working in larger firms, the motivation for engaging in rainmaking activity varies with each group.

> ***The chief advantage of being a sole practitioner is that you have full responsibility for setting the course of your practice, based only on your preferences and your business judgment.***

For law firm lawyers, the choice is between being a happier, wealthier, lawyer with more options or being a mere grinder who must rely on others for work and whose status at the firm can never be secure. For solo lawyers, the choice is a bit different: bring in the business and experience all of the benefits that accompany a full client roster and pipeline, or close up shop and look for a job with a law firm (or outside private practice). The simple truth is that a sole practice cannot survive without clients, and sole practitioners therefore must bring in new business.

Unlike lawyers in larger firms who have to answer to partners and management committees, solo lawyers themselves choose how to go about bringing in the business. As discussed previously, there is no one "right" way to get business, and as a sole practitioner, you have the freedom to use whatever method you prefer. You also have the flexibility to try new approaches without losing political capital if your plans go awry. Benefit from that advantage as you explore new ideas for business development. Although you may choose to pursue the tried-and-true routes to business development success, you can also try more novel approaches that might be discouraged in large firms.

For example, one of my coaching clients has been able to parlay connections with the Jaycees and Habitat for Humanity into a thriving family law practice. Another, though active in bar associations because he gets many referrals from lawyers, also hosts hunting weekends that function as both social and business opportunities. Both of these solos laid the business case for the approach and planned a test period, ensuring that they would not sink significant time or energy into an untenable approach. Adopt an entrepreneurial mindset and make it your goal to determine quickly what does and does not work for your practice. Devise a way to evaluate your success quickly so that if one approach fails, you fail quickly and then move on.

Equally critically, a solo can shift course at will. If a sole practitioner spots a hot new practice area or a new way to offer a legal service, he can move in that direction at a moment's notice. Lawyers in larger firms typically have to cut through levels of bureaucracy that dramatically slow the process, making a rapid response nearly impossible. Having the ability to react quickly to changed circumstances allows solos to be nimble in a way that their larger firm counterparts can only imagine. Consequently, be attuned to new developments and opportunities, and move quickly when you spot them. By using speed to your advantage, you may be able to become the frontrunner in your area, landing clients and business even before larger firms have the chance to convene the committees necessary to analyze how they might respond.

Sole practitioners must develop their credentials and credibility while developing relationships that will lead to new business and new clients. In practical terms, this dual–track responsibility often means that solos have fewer opportunities for time–intensive credential–building tasks such as writing, teaching, and speaking, at least until their practices are well established and profitable. Sole practitioners should therefore focus primarily on building relationships with clients and referral sources. The following are the top ten tactics that solo lawyers can use to expand their practices quickly.

Be attuned to new developments and opportunities, and move quickly when you spot them.

1. **Niche.** As discussed in Chapter 3, having a niched practice permits you to market exclusively (or at least primarily) to particular target audiences. Being a general practitioner makes business development more difficult because marketing to everyone requires a message that is sufficiently

diffuse to apply to everyone. Diffuse messages do not rule anyone out from your practice, but they tend to be much less effective because potential clients are unable to self–identify and self–qualify based on what you say.

When a potential client hears you speak or reads something you have written and recognizes himself in the descriptions and stories you share, he immediately realizes that you have the knowledge and experience to manage whatever legal situation he is experiencing. For example, if a potential client learns that you work primarily with corporations with annual revenue in the range of $500,000 to $5 million, focusing on licensing and intellectual property protection, that person will know immediately whether his company and legal needs fall within those parameters. If so, he knows you have something to offer to him, and he is likely to remember who you are because you have so clearly defined your practice.

If the same potential client learns that you represent businesses in licensing, intellectual property, corporation formation, general business litigation, shareholder and management issues, employment litigation, and employee benefits—and especially if the list continues on and on and could be summarized that you work with businesses on anything and everything—he will be much less likely to experience the same self–recognition in the description of your practice.

Claiming a niche allows you to create a well–defined marketing message. Potential clients will understand what you do and know whether they have legal needs that fall within the scope of your practice. You will be able to speak clearly and knowledgeably to the issues and opportunities within those areas. You will be memorable. When someone asks a referral source for the name of a lawyer who does a particular kind of work, that source is almost certain to recommend someone who specializes in the topic in question, not the lawyer who handles 20 areas of practice including that topic.

Although you will likely limit your practice to the areas you claim for your focus, you are not required to do so. If a potential client presents an intriguing matter that is outside your niche, but you are both interested and competent in the area, nothing prohibits you from taking on that matter. By creating a niched practice, you draw the boundaries of your preferred practice area and the heart of your expertise, but you may choose to step outside of those boundaries on occasion.

2. **Network extensively. Follow up. Network more.** The best way that a sole practitioner can grow her practice is to make one-on-one connections with potential clients and referral sources. For the purposes of this point, consider current and former clients to be potential clients (if your practice is amenable to repeat business) or referral sources if not. Make it your habit to appear regularly at the events your ideal clients and referral sources attend. Because slow yield activities are typically

too slow for sole practitioners who are just moving into rainmaking mode, you should focus on developing relationships that may yield business more quickly. A good rule of thumb: if you are not working on billable matters or critical administrative matters, you should be networking or following up with your clients and contacts. No lawyer can afford to languish in her office and hope that the telephone will ring; a sole practitioner must be out meeting people and making contacts so that she has the opportunity to return to her office and find messages waiting from potential clients wanting consultations. According to the quote attributed to Abraham Lincoln, "Things may come to those who wait, but only the things left by those who hustle."

> ***If you are not working on billable matters or critical administrative matters, you should be networking or following up with your clients and contacts.***

3. **Have a brilliant elevator speech.** Once you have identified your niche and resolved to network without ceasing, you must be sure that you have a brilliant elevator speech, sufficient to inform listeners about the scope of your practice and to draw them into conversation so that you can share appropriate stories about your work with clients and the good results they have experienced Review Chapter 12 for suggestions on creating a strong elevator speech, craft yours, and then practice it repeatedly. Ask your

mentor, your peers, your coach, your rainmaker group, and anyone else who might have good feedback to provide constructive criticism of your speech.

4. **Screen your clients carefully.** Chapter 16 suggests questions you should consider before accepting a client. As a solo, the quality of your clients will have significant impact on the perceived quality of your practice and on your quality of life. Accept engagements with good clients and good matters, and the reputation you develop will match. Moreover, to the extent that your clients become a referral source or a source of repeat business, you will benefit from accepting only the representations that are solid, with clients who act appropriately.

5. **Consider alternative billing arrangements.** The billable hour appears to be falling into disfavor, though it will likely continue to be among the most common fee arrangements for some time yet. Alternative billing arrangements can function, to some degree, as a rainmaking tool. Clients are almost always cost–sensitive, and though they may not select the least expensive lawyer, they will likely appreciate any effort you make to cap your fees or to share in the risk they assume. Consider what kinds of alternative arrangements you could offer to clients and how to make such arrangements appealing to your clients and profitable for you.

   The most common alternatives are flat fee

matters and contingency cases, but as a sole practitioner, you have the authority to come up with any alternative arrangement that is ethical and attractive. For instance, you could potentially arrange a flat fee with an increased payment for a speedy conclusion or special services rendered—if, for instance, rather than asking your client to come to your office to sign a document, you bring the document, notary, and witnesses to the client.

If you work with alternative arrangements, you will likely find, from time to time, that you lose money on a matter. When that occurs, evaluate what went wrong and account for it in the next billing arrangement. Your aim, of course, is to provide a service to your clients, but you must do so at a profit or you will be unable to continue. Your cash flow must be sufficient to support your practice's needs and your own, so you must also consider how to avoid dry spells in your income. You might consider cost retainers for contingency cases, for example, so that you are not put in the position of financing litigation. You will make financial mistakes along the way; nearly everyone does. Evaluate the finances of each representation when it closes and make adjustments as needed.

6. **Consider sharing office space with other (non–competitive) sole practitioners.** By office–sharing, you create a *de facto* referral group as well as a peer group to whom you can bring at least some of the questions that will arise about how to operate your practice. Those with whom you share office space

will reflect on your practice in some way: it would be unwise, for example, to concentrate your practice on special education matters and to share office space with a lawyer whose practice focuses on defending those accused of sexual offenses. Accordingly, as you consider office space, evaluate the synergy or discord that may exist among the practice areas represented.

Although you will generally find more success from sharing space with lawyers whose practices are compatible but not competitive with your own, the rules may be slightly different if you are a new practitioner. In that case, you might consider sharing space with a more senior lawyer in your practice area, with the intent of taking overflow assignments from that lawyer. By doing so, you may generate billings to supplement those you secure through your own clients. In addition, you would have the chance to learn from the senior lawyer, who may function as a mentor for you. You must, if you explore such a possibility, be transparent in speaking with the senior lawyer. Although she would almost certainly anticipate your reason for wanting to share space, you will benefit from demonstrating that you approach the subject in a candid and businesslike manner.

7. **If you work from home, consider where you will meet with (prospective) clients.** This issue crosses between business development and practice management and is critical from both perspectives. Working from home has become more and more

accepted, particularly since so much is now accomplished electronically. A practitioner no longer needs a law library composed of books; a computer and Internet access is sufficient for almost every research project. However, you must consider where to meet clients and potential clients, because the space in which you meet will send a message about your practice.

Some lawyers are comfortable meeting in the neighborhood coffee house, but some clients may find such a public, casual setting incompatible with the professionalism they expect to see. Others will view such a meeting spot as a comfortable accommodation to them and will pay no attention to whether the lawyer has a traditional office space for meetings.

If you plan to work from home because you do not wish to work in a traditional office suite setting, you should consider carefully whether to rent a single–room office in a business center. Offices in these centers are much less expensive than typical office space. The benefit of renting such a space lies not only in having an office and access to a conference room, but also in the option of having a receptionist answer your telephone line and having an office address that is not your home address. From a work/life balance perspective, you may also find that you prefer having a separate space you can use when you need to devote concentrated attention on a project. Depending on your approach to practice, each of these considerations may impact your business development success. Can one be a successful sole practitioner working from home? Absolutely. Can *you*? It depends entirely on your approach and your preferences. You should consider carefully what image you would like to cast for your practice, and then consider what physical space will best meet that image.

8. **Hire staff to whom you can delegate non–billable work.** Sole practitioners, like other lawyers, often struggle to handle all of the work, both billable and administrative, that accumulates every day in practice. As a solo lawyer, you have no one to whom to delegate billable work and thus no way to leverage your billable time. Moreover, every minute you spend on administrative work is a minute you cannot spend on billable work or on business–generating activity. Accordingly, you must seek to decrease the amount of non–billable, non–rainmaking activity that you do. The only practical way to decrease administrative work is to hire someone else who can handle it. Consider whether you would like to have a traditional W–2 assistant or whether you would prefer to explore working with a virtual assistant. See Part IV for further information about hiring and working with virtual assistants and delegating work to staff members.

> ***You must seek to decrease your amount of non–billable, non–rainmaking activity.***

9. **Surround yourself with mentors and advisors.** Lacking feedback from in–house colleagues, solo lawyers must receive business development support from a mentor or coach or rainmaking group. (You should find a source for practice management support as well.) Otherwise, you may find that it becomes difficult to see success (or failure) and you will begin to feel stuck.

   An outside perspective is helpful for casting light onto the opportunities that present themselves. One benefit of having a mentor, coach, or rainmaker group to call on for support is that you can share the opportunity you have identified, get feedback and ideas on how you might approach the client, position the service, or develop a new sub-focus in your practice. The more quickly you can respond to opportunities you see, and the more accurately you can tune your response, the better your return is likely to be. Do not permit yourself to approach practice as a lone ranger: have at least two or three trusted lawyers or marketers to whom you can turn for speedy, thoughtful feedback.

10. **Educate yourself as an entrepreneur and businessperson.** Law is both a profession and a business, and you must operate your practice accordingly. Few lawyers have business training, but because a sole practitioner is by definition a business owner, you would be well advised to acquire the knowledge necessary to manage your business well. Some knowledge of marketing is useful for rainmaking purposes, and business and

entrepreneurial skills underlie many of the approaches that you will employ for rainmaking. You need not attend business school, but do read a few books (both specific to law and not) addressing business, management, marketing, and sales. Read the recommended books on the Rainmaker Resource List (http://www.The Reluctant Rainmaker.com) to increase your knowledge of business topics.

By applying these top tactics, you will build a solid practice that will, over time, expand into a successful, satisfying, and sustainable practice.

Chapter 19

For Introverts

Introverted lawyers sometimes feel as if business development is an unrealistic goal for them, because they may not enjoy talking with strangers and feel they may not excel at building new professional relationships. The stereotypical rainmaker is someone who knows everyone, who has an active and enjoyable business social life, who operates with a never–met–a–stranger approach. Fortunately, that image is only partially accurate. Successful rainmakers may use a variety of business development strategies, "schmoozing" being only one possible approach.

Clients are, as already noted, by far the best source of new work. As a result, you should find ways to make all of your billable work dual–purpose—work undertaken to serve the client and undertaken in a way to develop the relationship with the client. This is not as difficult as it may initially appear. Take note of the suggestions in Chapter 2 about how best to serve clients, and remember to operate according to the so–called Platinum Rule: treat your clients as they would have you treat them. Most introverts do not find working with clients unduly daunting. The focus of most interactions is on the work, and if you engage in social interaction with a client, it rests on an existing relationship. Because you already represent the client and know, as a result, something about her and perhaps her business, building on that knowledge through appropriate questions will seem entirely natural. By the same token, you may be comfortable circling back to check in with former clients. In doing so, you create the opportunity for additional work or referrals, and you remain top–of–mind. Use your client interactions to forward your business development goals.

> ***Successful rainmakers use a variety of business development strategies.***

Introverts may find writing the most comfortable of the rainmaking tactics. If you are a natural and prolific writer, take advantage of your strength. Write articles for bar association newsletters and journals, client industry organization periodicals, and perhaps even your local newspaper. Prepare newsletters and client alerts that will keep your name in front of your contacts while providing useful information. Consider starting a blog, or become a frequent and articulate commenter on blogs that your ideal clients and referral sources will read.

If you write well and often, your name will frequently appear before those who may be in a position to direct business to you, and you may get increased search engine attention if your articles are published on the Internet. However, as described in Chapter 6, remember that writing tends to be a slow–yield activity. You can increase the chances of seeing measurable results by sending what you write to contacts and to clients, but few, if any, matters will come your way solely on the basis of written material.

Organizational involvement may also be a relatively comfortable activity, particularly since the work will be focused on creating some sort of product. You may find conversation easier to begin when it is centered on professional topics, and you will come to know your organizational colleagues over time. Find a group whose work interests you. Passion often overcomes discomfort, and if you are deeply intrigued by biotechnology, for example, the pleasure of participating actively in the work is likely to drown out any discomfort of joining an unfamiliar group. In addition, you can perform a tremendous amount of work by telephone and Internet interaction, with the result that an eventual in–person meeting is no longer a meeting with strangers but instead with professional colleagues you know well but have not yet met face–to–face. Because organizational involvement begins to build relationships, you may find greater resulting success here.

Networking is probably the least appealing task for introverts to undertake. Some lawyers find it easier to attend networking events with a colleague. If you fall into this camp, be sure that you and your colleague part ways during the event or tag–team to make new connections (by introducing one another, for example) rather than spending the bulk of the event talking to each other.

You might also consider setting a specific goal and promise yourself that you can leave, for example, after you engage in three substantive conversations. Some clients who have taken on this challenge discover that when they begin to compete against themselves in this way, and when they get engaged in conversation, they begin to enjoy the people they meet and may not want to leave even after accomplishing the stated objective.

One little–recognized fact bears some discussion here: introverts actually have an advantage in networking. Most everyone who attends networking events will harbor a "What's In It for Me" perspective, and some people will even behave accordingly, seeking to meet only "useful" people and to get as much as possible from each interaction. (These people typically fail miserably at networking because their insincerity is obvious.) Moreover, because a common error in networking is to fall into self–promotion (intentionally or otherwise), almost everyone has had the experience of talking with someone who seemed to be entirely self–absorbed. Those conversations are dull and almost never lead to good connections, and those tend to be the conversations that networkers dread.

If you are an introvert, you can distinguish yourself from pushy attendees by intentionally putting your focus on the people you meet. Ask questions about their business, how they came to attend the function, what other activities they have joined, and so on. By placing the spotlight on your conversation partner, you may feel less pressure to perform and may be able to relax into an ordinary flow of conversation. And while you may be concerned that holding other–focused conversations will not help you to advance your rainmaking goals, you may find that these conversations are actually the most beneficial. You will

> ***If you are an introvert, you can distinguish yourself from pushy attendees by intentionally putting your focus on the people you meet.***

probably endear yourself to your conversational partner.

Geri, a talented but shy tax lawyer, described talking for 35 minutes with an accountant and making sure that she left the focus of the conversation on the accountant during the entire conversation. When dinner was announced and she and the accountant parted ways to find their table assignments, the accountant told Geri that she was the most interesting person he had met in weeks!

Following that encounter and several subsequent conversations in which Geri was able to talk about her work, she and the accountant referred a number of matters to one another. Geri was able to tailor her comments in the subsequent conversations based on what she had learned during their first meeting, and so she focused on describing matters she had handled that mirrored the kinds of matters the accountant had alluded to previously. By remaining other–focused, Geri was able to feel more comfortable, to show her genuine interest in her conversational partner, and to discover unmet needs she was later able to show she could serve.

Finally, take note of the attitude you bring when you engage in client development activities. Do you dread them? If so, identify specifically what you dislike and find a way around it or a way to make the prospect more palatable. John, a self–identified "nice but introverted guy," detested the idea of business development because he felt like a fish out of water. When we began to explore the reasons for those feelings, John recognized that he believed that the goal of business development activities is to target people and use connections to get business, and he was uncomfortable with that approach. He wanted to be thoughtful to those with whom he came into contact and could not see a way to engage in rainmaking activity while meeting that objective.

When we discussed what he did for clients and the appreciation he sometimes received (as well as the satisfaction he felt in a job well done, even when it went unacknowledged by the client), John recognized that he was not using anyone and that providing legal services was in fact helping his clients. Moreover, he came to see that withholding his skill from someone who needed it would be destructive, not thoughtful.

Instead of viewing potential clients and referral sources as a "target" that, if "bagged," would generate extra income and other benefits for him, John began to view them as individuals who have or know others who have legal needs that he could meet. This recognition, while it might appear elementary, was a significant shift for John. It changed the attitude with which he approached client development activity from an uncomfortable "what can I get" to a thoughtful "what can I give" attitude.

John even altered the methods he used for business development to focus more on education and resource provision, in essence marketing his services by giving a taste of them. He felt aligned with this content–focused approach, which in turn made him feel more comfortable, which in turn made others feel more comfortable with him, and in the period of a few months John began to view rainmaking through an entirely different lens. He continued to struggle with some activities, such as networking among strangers when he felt a pressure to uncover their needs, so he focused on activities that were a better fit for him. When I last spoke with John, he had developed a reputation as a client service provider *par excellence* and brought in several new matters from and through existing clients.

PART IV

Rainmaker's Guide to Time Management

Chapter 20

Time Management

All lawyers struggle, to some degree, with time management. Regardless of your area of practice, the size of the firm in which you work, or the part of the country in which you are based, you are almost certainly familiar with the sinking feeling that accompanies the realization that you have more items on your "to do" list than time available to complete them. Billable work holds must–do status, as does some administrative work, and you likely have personal activities as well as family and friends clamoring for attention.

One of the most common objections to rainmaking is that it will take too much time. Many reluctant rainmakers worry that adding business development tasks to an already–packed schedule will simply be too much to handle. Even lawyers who are comfortable with business development sometimes put themselves onto a feast/famine cycle with new business. In this cycle, when they need new clients, they begin rainmaking activities and bring in the work—a feast! As the work begins to pile up, they cut back on rainmaking so that they will have more time for billable work, and at some point, they look up to discover that there are no clients in the pipeline—a famine! And then the cycle begins again. The mindset shared by reluctant and cyclical rainmakers is that business development requires too much time away from billable work.

The most successful rainmakers know a secret that seems to elude other lawyers: consistent marketing and business development activity will bring consistent results. (Seems simple, does it not?) In other words: do some rainmaking work every single day, whether your schedule is empty or booked completely. By integrating business development tasks into your everyday life, you will maximize the opportunity to grow a thriving practice and to terminate the feast/ famine cycle.

The most successful rainmakers know a secret that seems to elude other lawyers: consistent marketing and business development activity will bring consistent results.

To do so, however, you may need to change the way you operate with respect to time. This final section of *The Reluctant Rainmaker* offers ten time mastery approaches that rainmakers must accomplish. Observe these rules and you will find that you have more time for business development than you previously realized. As an added benefit, you will also discover that you use your time more effectively, and you will probably feel less stress as well.

Top Time Mastery Tactics for Rainmakers

1. **Start Each Day with the Most Important (Not Necessarily the Most Urgent) Task.**
2. **Plan for Periods of Concentrated Work.**
3. **Close Out Each Day by Planning for Tomorrow.**
4. **Manage Your E-mail – Do Not Allow It to Manage You.**
5. **Work with Your Circadian Rhythm, Not Against It.**
6. **Create Systems to Check in with Your Clients on a Regular Basis.**
7. **Create Systems to Manage Your Follow-up Contact.**
8. **Automate Your Outreach Efforts.**
9. **Become a Master Delegator.**
10. **Keep the Personal Touch Personal.**

Time Management vs. Time Mastery

Although most people talk about "time management," no one can actually manage time. The phrase "time management" suggests that if only we do the right things and we do them in the right order, or we add some trick that we are not using now, at last, magically, we will be able to manage time and therefore have more time. The truth is not quite so magical, however. We all have 24 hours in each day, whether we use it productively or fritter it away. However we choose to manage our time, the supply is finite. No one can create time, and whether time is managed well or poorly, no one can generate more than 24 hours per day.

Time mastery is a more appropriate phrase. Mastering time means accomplishing the right things at the right time. Through time mastery, you will get more done in the same number of hours, and, more importantly, you will ensure that you are getting things done in the proper order. You will serve your clients more effectively and more efficiently, which (even without other activity) may bring an increase in referrals. You will likely see an increase in clients hiring you again and again, if your practice is amenable to client repetition, because clients appreciate lawyers who use their time well. Client satisfaction with your work will go up, as will your own satisfaction.

Last but certainly not least, you will create more opportunities for rainmaking activity and you will see an increase in new cases and clients. You will no longer feel pressure to shortchange your client development time in an effort to get your billable work done. Instead, you will have prioritized your activities, delegated effectively, and leveraged your time well, and you will be able to dedicate time to the activities that lead to business.

All of these benefits, and more, flow from time mastery. Master your time so that you accomplish the things that need to be done when they need to be done, and you do them effectively. When you master your time, you increase the opportunities for making more money.

You feel less stress. You have happier clients. You build a sustainable practice.[4]

1. Start each day with the most important (not necessarily the most urgent) task.

Prioritizing your tasks is necessary to ensure that you do the right things at the right time. The Four Quadrant System, based on the work of Stephen Covey, A. Roger Merrill, and Rebecca Merrill in *First Things First*, sets up a useful distinction between urgent and important. "Urgent" refers to something that needs to be addressed immediately to avoid some negative consequence. A ringing telephone is urgent: you answer it or miss the call. A court hearing is urgent, because if you fail to attend and to be there on time, your client's interests (and your reputation or even freedom) may be compromised. "Important" tasks are those of great matter, significance, or value. In the Four Quadrant System, the juxtaposition of urgent and important (or the absence of either) determines the priority of each quadrant, as explained below.

The quadrants are represented as follows, with some examples of the rainmaking activities that fall in each quadrant:

---

[4] For much more information about time mastery, including step-by-step instructions on how to adjust principles to match your own practice and preferences, see *Seven Foundations of Time Mastery for Attorneys* by Julie A. Fleming.

I. Urgent and Important	**II. Not Urgent, But Important**
• Attending an industry organization meeting through which you have made profitable connections in the past • Preparing for today's client meeting • Reviewing notices of court filings to determine whether a client has been sued • Bringing in new business when in "famine mode" • Advising current client of recent developments in representation that require attention	• Creating a business development plan • Engaging in credibility–enhancing activity (writing and speaking) • Relationship–building with clients and key contacts • Preparing for next week's client meeting • Identifying potential referral sources • Bringing in new business when in "feast mode"
III. Urgent, Not Important	**IV. Not Urgent, Not Important**
• Meeting with a new contact without clear understanding of mutual or reciprocal interest or goals • Attending a networking event without knowing what kind of people you might meet	• Non–strategic social networking • Revising your business development plan to correct typos for the seventh time in six months (no substantive changes to the plan)

Quadrant I encompasses tasks that are both urgent and important. Most lawyers live in Quadrant I most of the time. Example include putting out fires and doing things that are deadline–based: drafting a brief just before the deadline, formulating an answer to a client's urgent questions, or preparing for a client meeting that is going to take place in about 20 minutes. Rainmaking activities in Quadrant I include attending meetings with the reasonable expectation of making good contacts, preparing for strategically planned meetings with clients or contacts, and all targeted rainmaking activity when you are operating in client famine mode. Learn to recognize Quadrant I activities as important tasks that are coming up on an urgent basis, when there is an imminent deadline or significant pressure to get the task done quickly.

Working in Quadrant I tends to be high–stress, because you have less time for reflection or revision. There is no way around spending some time in Quadrant I in the practice of law. We all know that doing a task shortly before a deadline can be, in some circumstances, effective. Doing so tends to be less effective for business development tasks, however, simply because time is required for strategic thinking and for finding the best approach. As you learn to prioritize according to the Four Quadrant System, though, you will begin to identify and work on important tasks before they become urgent, thus reducing your time in Quadrant I and moving into Quadrant II.

Quadrant II includes tasks that are important, but not urgent. Examples include strategizing and laying plans for an event or deadline that is not imminent. Quadrant II encompasses business development tasks that are at hand when you are working in a feast cycle and do not necessarily need to bring in more work. Creating a business development plan and laying the approach to reach the goals you set falls within Quadrant II: it is important work, but the motivation to accomplish it must be self–generated because (with the possible exception of an employer) no one will ever set a deadline for the completion of your plan.

Time spent in Quadrant II tends to be lower stress than that of Quadrant I, and the work produced in Quadrant II tends to be of higher quality because you have the opportunity to think it through more deliberately and with less pressure. Strategic thinking is, accordingly, best accomplished in Quadrant II. As you do more Quadrant II work, less Quadrant I work will be necessary, simply because you get the bulk of the work done before it becomes an urgency and develops into a high–stress, do–or–die scenario. Your rainmaking activity will be more considered and less of a seat–of–your–pants operation.

> ***The work produced in Quadrant II tends to be of higher quality because you have the opportunity to think it through more deliberately and with less pressure.***

Most Quadrant II activities can be done at any time, or in some instances (such as planning your career and setting professional goals), they can be skipped entirely without obvious consequences. If you do not intentionally carve out time to take care of Quadrant II tasks, they probably will not get done, or they will get done under the stress and pressure of Quadrant I, perhaps with poorer results than if they had been done in more reflective, deliberate Quadrant II time.

Finally, it bears noting that clients appreciate lawyers who work in Quadrant II. Excellent client service springs from Quadrant II operations. For example, all too often, a lawyer will send an important document to a client and request a fast response. Doing so is disrespectful of the client's time. It creates the impression that the lawyer was unable to plan sufficiently in advance and to complete the work early enough to allow the client time for meaningful review. Clients appreciate lawyers who handle matters effectively during an emergency, but they tend to resent those who act as if every event is an emergency. Living in Quadrant II will increase the quality of your client service, with the attendant benefits of increased referrals and repeat business.

Think of Quadrant III as a holding pen: many activities appear initially in Quadrant III because they are urgent, and only by addressing them can you discover whether they are also important.

Quadrant III includes tasks and activities that are urgent but not important. Some Quadrant III activities are immediately recognizable, such as a meeting you must attend that never produces results, and some activities are self–inflicted, such as hosting a contact for lunch without having a clear idea of what you would like to accomplish through that conversation. You might also think of Quadrant III as a holding pen: many activities appear initially in Quadrant III because they are urgent, and only by addressing them can you discover whether they are also important. For instance, a ringing telephone is urgent. It could be a telemarketer or it could be someone calling with the biggest case of your career, but you do not know which until you take the call. Everyone will spend time in Quadrant III due to required activities and the holding pen phenomenon. The key is to recognize when you are in Quadrant III and to minimize that time.

Quadrant IV encompasses tasks and activities that are neither urgent nor important. Non–strategic social networking that is ostensibly undertaken for business development purposes (such as spending hours "chatting" on Twitter, with no plans to turn the chatter into business activity) falls within Quadrant IV. The time is simply wasted. The same is true of repeated and unnecessary revisions of a business development plan. The activity is not urgent and it accomplishes nothing important. Because the time spent in Quadrant IV is unproductive, you will not feel better or realize better results by spending time in Quadrant IV. To get good rainmaking results, notice when you are engaged in a Quadrant IV activity and choose to do something different.

To get good rainmaking results, notice when you are engaged in a Quadrant IV activity and choose to do something different.

2. Plan for periods of concentrated work.

Create quiet hours for yourself when you will not be disturbed and can work with concentration and focus. Set aside the first few hours in the morning for this focused time, and let your assistant and colleagues know that this is your sacred work time. Unless a client calls with a genuine emergency, unless the court calls, unless a child or spouse calls with a crisis, you should not be interrupted. Be ruthless in protecting your time: if you fail to enforce that boundary, you will never get the uninterrupted time you need. Studies show that between 45 minutes and 90 minutes is the optimal amount of time for concentrated attention on work. Taking a short break to move around, to check e-mail, or to get a glass of water will function as a "reset" mechanism and prepare you for another block of concentration. If you can take an hour or two hours for focused work on your most important task, you will be much more effective—particularly if you do so first thing in the morning, or whenever your energy is at its natural peak.

Sara complained that she was ineffective in the afternoons at work. In a coaching conversation, she told me that she typically blocked out four hours each afternoon to focus on a large project. Halfway through the afternoon, though, she would get tired and easily distracted, and her work product suffered. I suggested that Sara experiment with dividing her afternoon into three 70–minute blocks, with ten-minute breaks for walking around, stretching, and listening to music that made her feel good. After trying her new approach for a week, Sara discovered that she was more effective even though she was actually devoting slightly less time to her work. She produced better work product and felt less distracted through the course of the afternoon. Sara's revised schedule allowed her to increase and focus her mental energy.

3. Create weekly and daily action lists.

At the end of each week, create the next week's action list. Maintain a prioritized running list of tasks and upcoming deadlines. Draw out the week's Quadrant I tasks first, and then determine which Quadrant II activities should be addressed this week. Think critically: your goal is to prevent any Quadrant II activity from becoming a Quadrant I activity. When you begin using this approach, you will probably need to clear the decks of urgent tasks before you can move into significant Quadrant II time. The sooner you can get to Quadrant II, activities, however, the sooner you will change the way you spend your time and the more benefits you will recognize.

Each evening, refer to your weekly action list to create your daily to do list for the next day. Again, make sure that the list is organized by priority so you know what your first task is each day, and ensure that you always have a business development task on your daily list. Using this approach will make it easier for you to begin working on your top priority every morning without needing to pause and consider what that top priority is. You will use your time more effectively and you will reap the maximum benefit from your early morning energy. Consider using a small piece of paper (or a 4″ x 6″ Post-it® note for easy visibility) so that you limit yourself to an attainable number of tasks to accomplish each day. Check your list to confirm that it includes only tasks (such as drafting a letter to opposing counsel) and not a project (such as drafting a motion for summary judgment); confusing the two means that your task list will include the same projects over a series of days no matter how doggedly you work, and you will likely find yourself demoralized and feeling that you have accomplished nothing even though you may have completed several tasks within the overall project. However you choose to keep your list, be sure you put it somewhere that you will see throughout the day to help you stay on track.

4. Manage your e-mail—do not allow it to manage you.

Check your e-mail only at predefined intervals, no more than once an hour. You will increase your productivity yet more if you decrease the frequency further and check e-mail only three times daily, ideally in the midmorning, midafternoon, and shortly before you leave your office for the day.

Consider not checking e-mail first thing in the morning. Many lawyers find that they easily get pulled into reading and responding to e-mail, handling "just one more thing" over and over until an hour or more has vanished in a whirlwind of necessary activity that is difficult to track and bill. Even more importantly, you may lose the high–energy morning hours to routine e-mail processing rather than using that time to get your top priority items accomplished.

If you have an assistant, allow him to access your e-mails and help him understand what is and is not an emergency. Ask your assistant to check your messages first thing in the morning and to monitor incoming e-mail on an ongoing basis in order to catch emergencies quickly. If you do not have an assistant who can perform this gatekeeping task for you, and if you receive emergency e-mails, get in the habit of scanning your in–box to look for emergencies but not reading or responding to non–urgent messages, no matter how tempting it might be to do so.

Alternatively, explore whether you can create an automatic reply notifying those who send you e-mail that you check e-mail messages only in the midmorning and midafternoon and requesting a telephone call if a matter demands a faster response. (If you are checking e-mail more frequently than two to three times a day, using such a message is unnecessary.) Even more effective is sharing that policy with clients and coworkers and explaining that you are more productive when you are not tied to your inbox. If you offer a cogent explanation, you may find that others will be happy to call you rather than send e-mail when they need a quick response.

Disable the audio or visual notification that you have received a new e-mail. Like a ringing telephone, an e-mail notification feels urgent even though the great majority of messages do not call for immediate review or response. More importantly, the notification itself (unlike a ringing telephone) is never urgent, because it merely advises you of an incoming message, which you can read at that moment or hours later. Eliminating the interruption caused by an e-mail notification will help you stay on track with your daily tasks, but responding slavishly to notification will keep your eye on the minutiae of your day and away from the important tasks you plan to accomplish.

5. Work with your circadian rhythm, not against it.

David, a senior associate, complained about his inability to make conversation with contacts during the breakfast meetings attended as part of his business development strategy. He always scheduled those meetings to begin very early (usually at 7 AM, and sometimes earlier) because most of his clients and contacts needed to be in their offices no later than 8:30. Twice a week, like clockwork, David would find himself sitting in a restaurant at 7 AM in the midst of a meeting or waiting for it to begin. Unfortunately, David is not a morning person. He dreaded those meetings. It would be a struggle for him to get enough sleep to feel sharp while talking with his breakfast partner, and he would often tear out of the house running late, which never set the stage for a great meeting. Week after week, David would wonder why breakfast meetings were so difficult for him.

During one of our coaching conversations, he decided to invite a few contacts to lunch or coffee, which he had resisted because, he said, taking time out in the middle of the day feels wasteful. But his contacts accepted the invitation, David felt rested and ready to engage fully in the conversation, and his results far outperformed his breakfast meeting results. He had more spur–of–the–moment ideas, he was able to shift more quickly to follow his companion's train of thought, and he was able to read reactions more accurately to help him guide his input. Success! David shifted to holding two lunchtime or coffee follow–up meetings each week. He compensated for the midday time out of the office by working later on those two days, and he was able to accomplish more of the objectives on his business development plan in a shorter time than he had while conducting breakfast meetings.

Shifting from breakfast to lunch meetings is a small tweak, but (as David's story shows) even a small tweak can produce big results. We all have a natural rhythm: times when we find it easier to concentrate, times when we are better at working on heavily analytical matters, times when we find it easier to socialize and have light conversation that can dive deeper when appropriate. Successful rainmakers know their rhythm and work with it, not against it. To the extent possible, design your days so that you do high–energy tasks when you feel high–

> ***Even a small tweak can produce big results.***

energy and lower–energy tasks when you are feeling more depleted.

6. Create systems to check in with your clients on a regular basis.

One aspect of your business development plan should speak to how you want to interact with your clients. How often will you communicate with them? How often will you invite clients to a social event? Your clients' preferences will, of course, inform your goals for client contact, and the events that occur in the course of a representation will affect how often you communicate with clients about matter–specific developments. By establishing a system for contacting your clients to check on their satisfaction, concerns, and new developments that may present an opportunity for you (or, through cross–selling, for a colleague), you will deepen your client relationships and raise the likelihood that you will discover any problems before they grow.

For maximum benefit, your client contact system should include regularly scheduled contact, contact triggered by events (holidays, perhaps your client's birthday, an annual golf tournament or music festival that you enjoy as a client development opportunity), and contact triggered by news about the client or legal developments.

Regularly scheduled contact with clients is important so that you can gauge your client's satisfaction with the representation and become aware of any problems. Most lawyers tend to assume that a client is satisfied with the lawyer's and firm's work unless the client says something to the contrary, but study after study reveals a significant gap between lawyers' perception of their clients' satisfaction levels and the clients' actual satisfaction. For instance, *How Clients Hire, Fire and Spend: Landing the World's Best Clients*, a 2006 study conducted by The BTI Consulting Group, Inc., found that "[o]nly 30.7% of clients are satisfied with their primary law firms," and that percentage does not appear to be on the rise. Communicate with your clients on a regular basis to find out what is and is not pleasing them about the service you are delivering.

Such conversations can be formal or informal. You should look to do an informal "spot check" every few months in a relatively active matter, perhaps at the close of a meeting or conversation to address the matter you are handling for the client. You might consider hiring a third party to conduct more formal client interviews to gauge their satisfaction with the firm. Appropriate third parties might be consultants who specialize in conducting client interviews, someone from your firm's marketing department, or a trusted legal assistant or paralegal. Although you may derive the most benefit from conversations that are a result of you conducting the interviews yourself, you may receive more helpful feedback from clients' candid comments to a third party. However you choose to conduct your formal client interviews, you should plan on checking in with clients at least once during the representation (and perhaps more than once for longer representations) and after the matter has concluded. Good questions to ask include:

Communicate with your clients on a regular basis to find out what is and is not pleasing them about the service you are delivering.

- What are we doing well?
- What could we be doing better?
- What could we do to make it easier to work with us?
- How could we make your life easier?
- How would you rate your overall satisfaction in working with us?
- What could we do to raise your level of satisfaction?
- What is most important to you in evaluating your level of satisfaction with us?
- Is there anything that we are not currently offering that might be useful for you and clients like you?
- Would you be willing to recommend our firm to others? Why or why not? What could we do to receive an enthusiastic recommendation from you?

You will realize an immediate benefit from checking in on your client's satisfaction, because you will get feedback that can improve your client relationships. The *caveat*, however, is that you must be prepared to act on the feedback you receive. While it may not be appropriate to implement every suggestion you receive in the course of client interviews, you must respond to every suggestion in some way, particularly when you receive feedback from a client in an ongoing representation. If you fail to do so, you will send the message that even though you asked what would make your client more satisfied, you do not care enough to act on or even acknowledge the suggestions you receive. That message could irreparably damage your relationship with the client.

In addition to improving your client relationships, checking on client satisfaction on a regular basis may yield new opportunities for additional business or for referrals. Tracy, a patent prosecutor, once asked a client (as a part of a routine satisfaction check–up) whether he would recommend her to someone else, and the client responded that he certainly would—and he pulled out his cell phone and proceeded to do just that! Tracy set an appointment at the client's recommendation, and she received a significant amount of work from that contact over the next few years. Although most lawyers talk about client satisfaction and do try to satisfy their clients, few make a concerted effort to check with clients throughout a representation, and those who do generate much good will from their clients.

Develop a system to make client satisfaction check–ups a regular part of your schedule.

Develop a system to make client satisfaction check–ups a regular part of your schedule. You might calendar them as soon as a new client hires you (perhaps for an informal check–up three and six months into the representation and for a formal client interview eight months later), or you might set a regular date (every quarter or so) when you will check in with every client to gauge their satisfaction. Having a regular schedule and, even more importantly, having a system to ensure that every client is included on the schedule will help you to manage your time well and to conduct these important conversations.

Event–triggered contact may be expected by your clients, and planning ahead will help you stay on schedule. For example, if you send holiday cards at the beginning of every December, you should schedule milestone dates leading up to the target mailing date to purchase the cards, prepare your mailing list, prepare mailing labels, sign the cards, and finally mail them. You will find it much simpler to accomplish the process if each step is noted on your calendar. In addition, by building in these systems, you may discover other opportunities. Perhaps instead of sending December holiday cards, you realize that if you start just a month earlier, you could send Thanksgiving cards instead and stand out from the crowd. Or you might decide to send something to mark the Fourth of July as well.

Be sure to mark your calendar for any other events that you want to observe. Client birthdays or significant anniversaries may offer good opportunities for you to follow up with your clients and former clients, for example. You might choose to send a small gift to clients when a new patent issues or when a financing deal is finally completed, or you might note the date on which tickets for a particular community event go on sale so you can invite a client to join you. When you create your "event trigger" system, start with the contacts you undertake now. Once that system is up and running, you will have the freedom to expand into new methods of outreach.

News–triggered contact will likely be your most common ongoing contact with former clients and can serve as an important interim contact opportunity with current clients. Watch for news about your client, your client contacts, your clients' industry, or anything that reflects upon or affects your client, and acknowledge that news in some appropriate way. You might see an article in your local newspaper, for example, announcing that your client or former client has just broken ground on a new construction project. Acknowledge that announcement by sending a note of congratulations. If you notice an article about an industry development that may impact your client, send a copy of the article along with a note offering to review the matter and provide some feedback or options. Alternatively, you might send an article that you have written addressing a recent regulation or case that affects your client.

Watch for news about your client, your client contacts, your clients' industry, or anything that reflects upon or affects your client, and acknowledge that news in some appropriate way.

Although you will be unable to schedule the news that provokes this kind of client contact, you can prepare a system so that you have a response mechanism arranged. (See *infra* for a discussion of how you can automate a system to help you find news relevant to your clients without having to invest tremendous amounts of time.) Your system could call for your assistant to order flowers if you see that a client's family member has died or to place a notecard with the relevant news story in your in–box for easier note–writing. The system you devise will be personal to you, and its primary function will be to create routine responses so that you never have to agonize about how to respond to news about a client. By creating a routine response, you remove guesswork, you develop a process, and you will become more systematized and thus more efficient in your news–triggered client contact.

7. Create systems to manage your follow-up contact.

Lawyers often find that the most challenging part of following up contacts is knowing what to do and when to do it. Chapter 12 discusses follow–up options at length, and you can refer to that chapter anytime you need to integrate some new ideas. After you have decided how you want to follow up with the people you meet and with those with whom you are working to build a stronger relationship, create systems to stay on track so that you no longer have to wonder when you should get in touch with one of your contacts. For example, you might decide to schedule a lunch meeting with your "A" list clients at least six times a year. Note on your calendar when you should get in touch to arrange the date, and note whether you should contact the person by e-mail, telephone, or otherwise. (You can even make it a point to vary your mode of contact each month so the process does not feel mechanized.) If you make arrangements by e-mail, save your draft as a template that you can reuse in the future. When your reminder pops up, simply pull up the template, revise to include a current greeting and appropriate date suggestions, and send it to your contact.

Other examples of follow–up systems that my coaching clients have created to follow up with their contacts:

1. Select two days a week for contact lunches (or other meeting times) and make it a part of your Friday routine to fill those slots.
2. Follow up with new contacts via e-mail within 48 hours of your first meeting.
3. When you return from a conference, give all of the

business cards you have collected to an assistant for scanning. Review the cards and select those with whom you wish to follow up, those whom you had promised to send a resource, and those who had promised to send a resource to you. Have your assistant send the promised resource, and send a template–based e-mail to the other recipients to follow up. Deadline for completion: five days following return.

4. Create a list of contacts with whom you would like to have coffee or lunch; reach out to those contacts to request the meeting and to express your interest in catching up, and ask your assistant to coordinate the appointments.
5. When you are preparing for a trip, ask your assistant to gather a list of contacts who live in the destination area. Call or e-mail those you would like to see beforehand to make arrangements, and take a list of telephone numbers with you so you can call to say hello while you are in town.

You must determine whether each (or any) of these systems will be appropriate for your personality and practice. Although you should not create so many systems that your follow–up becomes unduly complicated, you will likely find that incorporating several systems into your routine will allow you to stay in touch with your connections on a more regular basis.

8. Automate your outreach efforts.

The Internet has made outreach simpler than ever before. As you read about new websites or receive website–generated contacts, watch for new developments that may make your life easier when it comes to nurturing your contacts. Technology changes quickly, but the following automated systems may be useful for you.

News alert services (such as Google Alerts, Metion, Talkwalker, and Newsle) automate the process of searching for news that is relevant to your clients and contacts. These systems are free and easy to use. To begin, make a list of the people, companies, industries, and keywords you would like to search. If, for example, you represent a mattress manufacturer, you might list the names of each of the major companies, the names of their officers and key employees, and words like mattress and bedding.

Coming up with your list of search terms is the hard part, but you can set up the alerts very quickly. Bear in mind that you may want to tweak your searches as you see the results being delivered to you. You might also make it part of your system to enter each new client's name as a search term, and plan to reevaluate your searches at least quarterly. Once you determine what your search terms are, you might consider delegating the set–up for the alerts to someone else.

Create e-mail filters to avoid being overwhelmed with information flooding your in–box. If you use a folder–based e-mail system, create an alerts folder and set aside the time to go through that folder every day. Although you will find pearls in the alerts that you receive, much of the information you receive will be old news or unhelpful for purposes of staying in touch with your clients or contacts. Daily review is critical (by you or, preferably, by an assistant) because you may get enough results returned to you that you will be overwhelmed if you fail to review the alerts frequently.

By automating your search for interesting news and developments, you will generate a steady stream of information that you can use to stay top–of–mind with your clients and contacts. Alerts do the background work for you, if you set the searches correctly, and by reducing the time you must spend finding helpful information, you increase the amount of time you can spend communicating with your contacts and delivering that information.

SendOut Cards facilitates sending personalized greeting cards and gifts through the mail, making it as easy as sending an e-mail. When you use SendOut Cards, your recipient will receive a standard–sized greeting card with a stamp on the envelope (no postage meter), with the envelope and the message inside the card printed in a "handwritten" font. If you would like, you can even arrange for the card's message (but not the envelope) to be printed in a font matching your own handwriting.

You can also choose to send a gift, such as a Starbucks® gift card or gourmet brownies. SendOut Cards features thousands of cards to choose from and makes the process of selecting a card, preparing a message, and having it mailed take less than three minutes and cost less than $2. Note, however, that some recipients may have a strong, negative reaction to finding a facsimile of a handwritten card in the mail. With this tactic, as any other, you must know your audience. Visit http://www.sendoutcards.com to learn more.

Visit the Rainmaker Resource List (http://www.TheReluctantRainmaker.com) for additional online resources that will assist you in automating your outreach to clients and contacts.

9. Become a master delegator.

Some delegable rainmaking tasks are obvious: researching meetings you might attend, assistance with formatting written marketing materials, and making reservations for lunch meetings are common examples. However, you can also create systems that allow for delegation where it would otherwise be difficult to do so. First, notice what tasks you do repeatedly and consider how you might create a system to make the task routine. Having created that system, look to see whether some or all of it may be delegated. For example, scanning industry newsletters and business news for information germane to your clients can be time–consuming. However, once you have identified the relevant industries and search terms, you can use assistants or automated alerts to cull down to the key articles you should read.

Notice what tasks you do repeatedly and consider how you might create a system to make the task routine. Having created that system, look to see whether some or all of it may be delegated.

Your system for locating relevant information includes the identification of terms and phrases that catch your eye and the sources you review to find that information. You might find it possible to delegate the search keyword identification to another lawyer familiar with the client or matter, or you might prefer to do this set–up work yourself. You may delegate, however, the search itself and perhaps even a preliminary review of results to an assistant.

Once you begin assessing your daily activities with a critical eye, you will begin to discover many tasks that you can delegate. If you find that you hold on to more of your routine rainmaking preparation work than you should, and if you have a sharp assistant and/or junior colleague, consider asking them what you could be delegating. You might be surprised what they see and how much they can handle. Finally, whenever you notice that you are doing something not within your special expertise, question whether you should delegate that task.

If you find that you have enough delegable work to keep someone occupied for a few hours a month but not enough to hire an (or another) assistant (or if you would simply prefer not to incur the expense and commitment of an employee), consider hiring a virtual assistant or an intern. Virtual assistants ("VAs") are ideal to help with any task that does not require an assistant's physical presence. While that restriction may seem limiting at first, you will quickly recognize that almost anything can be accomplished remotely. Most routine administrative tasks, such as transcribing dictation, scheduling appointments, and making travel arrangements, can be completed by a VA just as easily as they can by someone sitting in the next office.

To find a VA, look for a clearinghouse organization (such as AssistU) that allows you to search for assistants with the kinds of skills you require. You can even find a VA with legal experience or expertise as an executive assistant. Be sure to interview several candidates and to ensure that the VA you select has the skills you need, especially if he will deal with your clients and contacts.

Another option for limited extra assistance is to hire an intern from a local college. An intern is a good choice for routine tasks that do not require much knowledge about the law or the operation of a legal practice, such as preparing holiday cards that you have signed and envelopes for mailing. You achieve the double benefit of getting the help you need and acting as a mentor, especially if your intern is considering a legal career. To find an intern, check with local schools or post an advertisement on Craigslist. Of course, you must interview candidates carefully and ensure that your internship comports with employment law, but you can find quality people using either route.

10. Keep the personal touch personal.

Know when you may and when you should not automate and delegate your rainmaking activities. For example, you might find that SendOut Cards offers an easy and appreciated way to send a follow–up note after you have had lunch with a contact. Using SendOut Cards to send an automated note and gift card to thank a client for retaining you on a matter that will generate substantial legal fees is likely not appropriate. A client who has had extensive contact with your assistant may gladly receive a call from her to schedule a time for a lunch meeting with you, but a contact who has never spoken with your assistant might find the same kind of call to be an arrogant delegation.

Give thought to the tasks you choose to automate or delegate. Moreover, if you choose to delegate a task, be certain that the person to whom you have delegated it is capable of carrying it out with skill and due care. Delegation and automation may both be used effectively and graciously, and both may be misused in a way that will disrupt rather than develop relationships.

How Does This Approach to Time Management Assist a Reluctant Rainmaker?

If you convince yourself that you lack the time to engage in business development activity and find it more comfortable to be a grinder, you will experience fewer and fewer professional options as your career progresses. By recognizing that certain time mastery tactics can assist with your business development work, you will understand how to create more time for rainmaking activity. Equally importantly, you may add a new approach to managing your billable work and improve not just your business development work but your billable and personal time as well.

Conclusion

The foregoing chapters have presented many ideas for business development approaches. If you select even a few and apply them strategically and consistently, you will bring in new business. Remember that some practices are more amenable to bringing in a quick spike in billable work than others, and judge your results accordingly. Indeed, you might even consider how to balance your practice so that you have expertise in substantive areas that have different growth patterns and that will respond differently to economic downturns.

What you do next will determine your success. If you put this book on your shelf, along with others about rainmaking, and fail to implement what you have learned, nothing will change. As we have all heard, "the road to hell is paved with good intentions." To bring in new business, you must marry strategy and consistent action. The intention to make rain is important but, by itself, impotent.

How Can We Work Together?

For most, this book plus a mentor or two or a rainmaker group will be all you need to get started with rainmaking. Some, however, may be interested in more intensive work, either to accelerate results or to overcome specific challenges. If you are interested in working with me, one–on–one or in a group setting, please contact me by sending an e-mail to julie@LexInnovaConsulting.com or by telephoning 800.758.6214, ext. 1 (within the U.S.) or 404.954.2523 (outside the U.S.).

Julie A. Fleming, principal of Lex Innova Consulting, helps lawyers to create and implement innovative business development plans. She is the author of three books (*The Reluctant Rainmaker: A Guide for Lawyers Who Hate Selling*, *Seven Foundations of Time Mastery for Attorneys*, and *Legal Rainmaking Myths: What You Think You Know About Business Development Can Kill Your Practice*), as well as numerous articles on topics such as business development, practice management, work/life balance, and leadership development. Before launching her consulting business, Julie practiced law for over a decade in firms of 3 to more than 2100 attorneys, focusing on patent litigation. Julie's work has appeared in diverse publications including *The Practical Lawyer* (ALI CLE), *Trial* magazine (American Association for Justice), *The Bencher* (American Inns of Court), *ABA Now* (American Bar Association), and *The Glass Hammer*.

Julie is a Fellow of the American Bar Foundation and most recently served as Vice Chair of the ABA Section of Science and Technology Law. Previous American Bar Association appointments include: Editor-in-Chief of The SciTech Lawyer; Chair of the Life Sciences and Physical Sciences Division and Biotechnology Committee; Council member for the Section of Science and Technology Law; member of the Special Committee on Bioethics and the Law; and member of the Standing Committee on Ethics and Professional Responsibility.

Julie earned her J.D. in 1993 from the Emory University School of Law, her B.S., *magna cum laude,* in biology in 1998 from Georgia State University, and her B.A. in 1990 from Vanderbilt University, and a certification in leadership coaching from Georgetown University in 2006. She is registered to practice before the United States Patent and Trademark Office and is admitted to the bars of Georgia, the District of Columbia, and Florida.

Made in the USA
Charleston, SC
28 March 2014